# SLAYING YOUR DRAGONS

# Slaying Your Dragons

LIVING THE LIFE
YOU ALWAYS
WANTED

## Michael Kane

Mogul Force LLC

# Contents

# Copyright

# Dedication

This book is dedicated to my wonderful wife Sandra and to our children and family. And to you the readers, may you be blessed somehow from the content of this book.

# The Struggle Is Over

## The Struggle is Over

You Can Win the Fight!

You have the Power and Control!

You May be Divided Today be Whole Tomorrow!

# Preface

**Origin**

There are differences of opinion as to the origin of slaying dragons. Was it just a clever idea or was it a practice? As they say, fiction or nonfiction, what or who to believe?

One viewpoint is based on pure mythology, fantastical tales of creatures that breath fire and that fly faster than Superman, For you diehards, it's certain that the man of steel falls under mythology. Back to dragons. Dragonist, (my term for those folks into dragons), dragon lovers or aficionados believe these creatures are sentient beings that think, reason, and calculate, brilliant in some regards. Did I leave out cunning and nearly indestructible?

Other opinions involve religion or secular thoughts that a hero arrived to save the day. Stories that pit good men versus evil dragons. These typically end where a hero slayed the big, bad dragon and received some type of reward. I imagine there are some folks who think dragons should be a protected species. It would be disingenuous of me to support the side that dragons are harmless, misunderstand and are worthy to be saved. The title and basis of this book speaks for itself of where I stand.

Let's delve a bit deeper on one particularly interesting origin story. This imaginative fable or possible historical account is about the legend of Saint George and the dragon. Apparently, back in the third century there was a very bad dragon that demanded the villagers pay tributes in the form of livestock and trinkets. After some time, the livestock and stuff were all gone, and the only tribute left were people. So, the villagers had a lottery where human sacrifices were selected.

This is one lottery you hope your number was not drawn. After satisfying the dragon with human sacrifices the beloved daughter and princess of the king was chosen. The king begged the people to allow his daughter a waiver for being the next sacrifice. The people refused and took the princess to the area for sacrifices.

The dragon eventually came for his dinner. Fortunately for the princess, Saint George happened to be passing by and confronted the dragon and killing it saving the princess. Whether you believe this story or not it helped support the theme of light versus darkness essentially good versus evil with good winning.

Are dragons real?

This book uses dragons as metaphors for something not good for us. This something could be making bad decisions, missed opportunities in your control, self-sabotage, back stabbing and experiencing downright evil. In the end dragons as I reflect on them are spirits that we need to drive out of our lives because nothing good is coming from them.

In answering the question, you be the judge.

# 1

# Introduction

**Congratulations!**

You are on your way to defeating the mighty, scary, and ferocious dragons in your life. It is never too late to take back control of your life. No matter how powerful the dragon, you are more powerful. You will discover your potential and authority in this book. A life worth fighting for is a life worth living. My friends, the dragon of fear is a common enemy. This dragon is the most dangerous and cunning. Its close cousins, dragons of procrastination and dissatisfaction are willing, able, and very ready to destroy your life. There are thousands of these creatures planning to kill, steal and destroy. All dragons are not alike, so one size solutions do not fit all circumstances.

This book will help you in both your personal and professional lives. Yes, at home or work the dragons will interrupt the achievement of your goals, dreams, and conquests. Your nightmares are the end result of dragon intervention.

Business owners or corporate titans are not immune from the dragon's bite. You want to increase revenues, productivity and profit then slay your dragons before they take you down leaving only faint memories of what could be.

Why did I choose dragons as a metaphor for the things troubling and hindering your success?

Well, dragons represent oppression, danger, the ability to create unbridled fear, generates weakness in their nemesis namely us, they take and overpower, and they destroy hope. They're dream killers. These dragons can be in your head, or negative circumstances in real 2D or people in your life on a personal or professional level. Whatever or whomever the source of your dragons you must seize stewardship of your life and not acquiesce your destiny, purpose, and happiness any longer to others dominance by will or peaceful measures. No one has a right to dominate you except for you. Yes, there are bullies and worse in this world. I will refrain with more aggressive language, it's hard to not use other words that may be more appropriate. These dragons may walk near us, live and work amongst us. If you live long enough you will encounter dragons a plural for sure.

**Warning!** If you are a dragon, please close this book immediately; you are about to be banished.

This book will help you identify the things in your life that are holding you back. Once you identify the obstacles you must decide for yourself if moving forward to reach your goals and dreams is worth fighting. If the answer is yes, then taking action is part of the next step. However, before you take action you must prepare and plan your strategies and tactics to get you there.

As I mentioned there are thousands of dragons. Many of them are in the form of phobias. Later in the book, I listed a few phobias but they are numerous, too many to name in this book. But once you gain the tools and weapons of defense under your belt you will be able to meet the other dragons head on. Watch them fall one by one. You were born to be successful. Don't allow anyone to knock you down literally or figuratively ever again. I used to allow that in my life but no more. And stop making excuses for people that do things to harm you. People show you who they are every day. You just keep your eyes open and mind on high alert to recognize it. It is what we do not what we say.

Now, some of these dragons are of our own making. I know I probably lost a few people who continue to make poor decisions and then blame others for their repeated mistakes. Okay, I am sure the haters are hating now. Remember the funny comedian, Flip Wilson? He appeared in the 1960's and 1970's, on numerous television shows and his own show many years ago. He was famous for the line "the devil made me do it" as himself or his favorite character. He dressed as a female character called Geraldine. When someone asked, "why did you buy the dress?" Geraldine would say, "the devil made me buy the dress." Hilariously delivered but mocked the ready to go response that someone else is responsible rather than accept responsibility. If you are late for work and your boss asked you, why are you late then now you have a ready to go response, "the devil made me late". May not fly but a unique excuse.

Seriously, it is important that we be honest in our assessment of the source of these dragons. This will be necessary to enable our efforts to eradicate them from our lives. It is quite possible to eliminate dragons only to see them return with a stronger vengeance if you avoid transparency as to their source of origin. One of the first steps in conquering something is to acknowledge there is a problem and secondly that we need help.

Disclaimer: this book is not a cure for all. Some issues may require a licensed professional and expert. So, this book is not meant to undermine those that are in the business of helping someone overcome a situation or challenge. I encourage you to seek assistance. This book is a primer on dealing with life in a productive way. Slaying your Dragons is meant to be motivational and hopefully inspirational.

I wish you all well in your pursuit of success, happy journey!

# 2

# Rise Up

**Dragons Step Down Achievers Move Up!**

I did much soul-searching as to which road to take in composing this introductory chapter. First impressions mean everything, right? Well, for the sake of argument the answer will be resounding - yes for sure. I wanted my readers to know that I had something meaningful to say by demonstrating my intentions. My focus was and always will be the well-being of my readers, clients, friends, family and to those who desire to raise the bar and truly experience life to the fullest. I reflected on every word as I wrote to get my story from my head onto the page.

Is my life a reflection of what Utopia means to me? Am I finally arriving to my destination, the destination of fulfillment, of the truest form of happiness ... is it time to celebrate?

In summary, my life has been greatly impacted by my choices, things out of my control and life altering experiences.

Hmm, have I totally arrived to my destination? No, but inching closer each day. I tend to think of life as a traveling roadshow. Perhaps I am thinking too deeply, maybe over-thinking as the mere self-questioning builds a pressure, a torrential swell of emotions ripping through the very fabric of my mind, body, and spirit.

Take a break I said to myself given the daily grind, work, family, children and a plethora of activities that occupy over two-thirds of my day. Just live each day as it comes soaking in the positive substance of my life I said to myself. Scrapping off those negatives that keep pulling me down that want to silence any joy entering my mind. Back to the question have I arrived? To double-down, no, not in the sense we typical mortals really mean. See, I believe the living of a life is more a journey than a destination. Do we achieve goals, objectives, and New Year's Resolutions? Surely, we do. Good for those that achieve whatever it is they want to achieve. I am very thankful for the life I presently lead.

My view of life is simple. I create a plan for the day, for the week, for the month, for the year and so forth. I get up in the morning, get ready for the day and execute my plan for that day not worrying about the plan for tomorrow, for the week and on and on. As I sojourn hoping, praying, and working my plan, I may have to retool or modify that plan as stuff happens, things may not go as to plan. The point? At the end of the day, I celebrate the accomplishments for that day no matter big or small. No matter trivial or extraordinary the achievement might be. On certain days, washing and drying the dishes may have been one of the best accomplishments in terms of closure for that particular day.

What many of us do is knock ourselves down long before any negativity generated by others are hurled our way. See, what we must do in my opinion is to raise the victory cup each time a day passes with some level of marked achievement in our grasps. Living on purpose, wow, a grandiose idea or is it just a nice clever sub-title to this chapter? Yes, it does sound powerful indeed with a drum roll built in its name. But it is much more than a title but more so a way of life. I encourage readers to use it as a mantra, a prayer and piece for meditative thought. A life with intention is what it means. True circular reason, I get it. We know what it means when we say," I did it intentionally or even I did it on purpose. However, when it comes to living our lives and not dealing with objects or situations the term or phrase become quite nebulous.

It took me a bit of time, some time well spent, and time well wasted to figure out my purpose or meaning in this thing called life, but I was not alone as many flounder discovering the truth later in life. Now, true, some people just seem to migrate naturally toward their vocation and know who they are and what they were designed to be or do in life. Good example, my older brother knew he wanted to be an attorney at the age of 15 years. That was great for him as he was laser focused on the path to get him from thinking about it to neophyte to expert in the legal arena. In reflection, I did have some clues and opinions about the direction I should take however, the vision was kind of fuzzy filled with self-doubt and fear. Ah, yes,  my dragon is taking hold.

As time progressed, I became focused not only on the desire to succeed but the road to take. I still had issues with the timetable of my deliverance from mediocrity and over-listening to well-intentioned advisors to play it safe and not take any risks. Let's stop for a moment with this thought. What is playing it safe mean? Playing it safe to me in my earlier years was to slam the brakes on any idea of being me and living out my dreams of what success was to me.

What about risking taking? In my opinion, earlier on in my life, this was another way of saying to go the traditional route no matter your calling, attending college and obtaining a nice conservative job and perhaps waste time while losing all hope, all the real vision for my life. A mouthful for sure. Of course, there is nothing wrong with this route if it speaks to the intended vocation you set forth, to strive for and to realize.

In fact, in my later years I became more appreciative for having the parents I had to push me to obtain a business degree as I wanted to be in business for myself one day. But at the time I did not see the full extent to what my parents meant by play it safe. Playing it safe to them was academic; to gain knowledge by earning a college degree and then gaining real-world experience. What about those people that never went to college or dropped out and made it big? Well, great for them. Each person's path is just that, their path.

Attempting to replicate or follow a path other than your own will likely lead ultimately in disaster. Short-termed gain may be a welcomed guest for a while but sacrificing a long-term successful future is a regret many endure because of being too anxious or envious of what someone else achieved in the manner they achieved their dream.

Too be clear, we all have skills and talents that were nurtured or innate from the womb. That said, from birth to adulthood the primary objective is to find our truth of what we should be doing and who we should be. If we stand still to listen to that inner voice or research or challenge ourselves perhaps, we can minimize or even eliminate wasted time chasing a false dream. Perhaps instead of asking little Johnny what you want to be when you grow up instead ask what should you be as you grow up? You see, every expert knowledge that exists in our head or skill we seem to be a virtuoso does not mean this is what we were meant to do with our lives. This does not mean that you should not reap the financial benefits from any God-given talent or enable a serious hobby for prosperity.

Living your purpose runs deeper than the flesh. It penetrates the muscles and bones down to the cellular level, our root core spirit level. Many people that invoke some talent they acquired or higher-level education or lucrative vocation for some reason have no joy, no contentment, and no peace. For some individuals, attempted suicide or suicide was a response for an unhappy existence despite the fame or riches. While others live out their lives miserable forsaking any hope of doing what they were supposed to do acting out a tragic play like Shakespeare's Romeo and Juliet, until their final curtain call.

This book was designed to initiate the fire in its readers. I said, "the fire" rather than "a fire" because "the fire" is just that your catalyst for change or transformation that can only belong to you. As I climbed the so-called corporate ladder, I was interviewing for positions left and right devoid of soul-searching and discerning if that position was right for me or not. That is until I had an epiphany or aha moment. At some point in my career, I felt empowered to say no to just any perceived opportunity that crossed my path. So, I did just that I began to decline offers after much gut-wrenching thought, meditation, and prayer. I learned that everything that appears good may not be good or right for me.

Let's extend this conversation to other areas of our lives. For example, the topic of relationships creeps up in my thoughts. More specifically, who to marry or who our significant other should be. This subcategory of purpose is key to our daily happiness in general and even more so economic happiness. Back up for a moment. Our lives are made up of a series of choices. We make a choice on what we eat for breakfast, and which suit or dress to wear today. These choices are indeed important. However, there are rankings of degrees of choices on how deep they influence our lives. They play out in a cause-and-effect battle to elevate or destroy.

To the original point of domestic relationships and who

to marry. If you choose incorrectly, your joy will turn into a famine of the heart and much pain and anguish to follow. Part of our living on purpose is to select the right mate if that is our purpose or design. The right mate will help elevate your life to a level you may not reach on your own. This is not to say every person on earth must be with someone to achieve great levels of success. Furthermore, I am not just referring to economically but emotionally and psychologically as well. In fact, some people's calling is not being with anyone.

My point is if you feel compelled to do so, choose wrongly and much grief is waiting for you. Not to say every bad relationship is sponsored from the gates of hell. Some people should not be together for a variety of reasons. They do not have much in common, i.e., interests, hobbies, movies, sports etc. There is no chemistry on both a physical and/or emotional level. Compromise only works if these other factors are met. Please note, I periodically fall into side bars regarding commenting on relationships because they are usually the number one dream and life killer if not successful. Nevertheless, more on relationships in another chapter.

We so far briefly touched on how our purpose influences our vocation and domestic relationships. It also will influence the school we attend, the business partner or investors we seek to start our business. Whether we travel abroad or hop the bus to only the next city over is impacted as well to the direction we take in life. Let's not forget the children to have or not to have which tends to be included in who we marry or not.

So, in other words, living on purpose is speaking to the type of choices we make but more so to what road should or must we take to realize our life goals. It is a good idea to seek wise council. However, the best counsel in the end will be your heart and must-haves at your soul level. I would urge you not to chase dreams that don't belong to you. You may gain money, prestige, and accolades, but lose inner peace and much joy. The expression losing one's soul comes to mind.

# 3

# What Time is It?

**Dragon of Chronophobia (Time)**

Prior to jumping too much into the meat of the book, I thought it appropriate to first write about a subject that is very important to the scope of not just this book but a subject that heavily impacts everyone on planet earth. There are a few things on this earth that all the money in the world cannot buy. The first thought that comes to mind is that thing called love. Yes, "you can't buy real love". So true but in this chapter good guess but wrong answer.

How about a nearly priceless Leonardo da Vinci? Or the Hope Diamond? Or, better yet, what about the extremely rare Kadupul flower found in forests of Sri Lanka where it only blooms at midnight and perishes before the dawn? Now that's very rare without argument.

Again, incorrect to all the above. Okay you must be contemplating where is this trivia game going. Yes, I have an unfair advantage as the author of this game. What I am referring to is the great equalizer of the Universe – where the poorest people are matched evenly with the likes of the wealthiest people, i.e., Jeff Bezos, Amazon king, Elon Musk, Tesla visionary, Warren Buffet, Berkshire Hathaway investment guru and Bill Gates, former Microsoft founder and CEO.

If you haven't guessed yet, drum roll please … quite simply your money cannot buy the most precious commodity we call "Time".

Each day as we begin the new day by stepping out of the bed, the clock continues to tick, tock, tick, tock advancing by the second, the minute and the hour. All of us without exception is delivered the same opportunity with the gift of time. Actually, the clock starts ticking even before we awaken to live out our new day. Regardless of if you are rich or poor, whatever your background, ethnicity, culture or race the slate resets blank every 86, 400 seconds.

Okay, so how do you get more of it? The truth is you can't, no one can expand the time we're given. But you say, "so and so at my job seems to get all his or her work done way before I take my first break, how do they do it?" Or "I have to pick up Susie from the babysitter, then go grocery shopping then work on that report I didn't finish at work and on and on etc." "Is this you? The bottom line is "I just don't have the time".

Needless to say, we must become more productive with

the time given us. This can pertain to our jobs or personal lives. Although the emphasis on many articles and books chooses the former or latter, my mission is to focus on both as a life/work balance issue. Let's face it, we don't live in a vacuum, usually one or the other demands our attention either on a rotating basis or worst-case scenario – simultaneously besieging our precious time with stress and guilt. The end result when we need to go left, we go right and vice-versa.

Life and work balance issues are not the easiest to resolve given we owe are utmost loyalties to both our workplace and our families. I want to talk about the life part first in terms of family. I do realize some readers don't have children but stay with me on this journey as I know your situation may include eldercare or tending to hobbies or helping others in need. On one hand our responsibilities as parents or guardians are the most sacrosanct of all duties, we are called upon to perform in this precious life we live. Having and raising children is one of the best moments a father or mother or guardian can experience. From newborns to adulthood our duty never stops only mutates to the ratio of child to parent.

As a father and for years a single parent at that, I experienced both joy and heartache as I attempted to do my best. Yes, I helped with the homework, putting food on the table, laughing, crying, consoling if the child is ill or disappointed and attending school and extracurricular events. Very time consuming to say the least. As you deal with the home life you undoubtedly have the job to contend with as you alternate allegiances when your loyalty is challenged by either family or employer. The workplace demands on your time are not any easier at times.

As you are aware, without the needed stable paycheck; life would be a lot worse. As employees regardless of the title or level we owe a duty to perform at the highest level possible. Of course, professional goals, domestic situation and age play a part on our level of attention to family and job. Let's take it in perspective. For example, when we graduated from college perhaps still living with our parents in our early twenties beginning our sojourn in the workplace we were at a point in life where there were no diversions to our attention away from work. I will insert myself as an example. As I started out in the workforce single and childless, I could work ungodly hours at work. To build my financial empower I accepted every opportunity to work overtime and special assignments that would engulf any thought of availability of or for personal time.

In fact, I worked two jobs to accelerate my progression toward obtaining as much money as I could. Over and above the increased income I was observed to be an employee that others could count on at a moment's notice given no other responsibilities in my life. What personal life? Didn't exist at the time. Like the O'Jays' song, "For the Love of Money" that was a focus and building credibility as a hard worker as well. I had extreme flexibility with my time and the willingness to commit to 100 hours to the workplace. But then something happened.

My interests away from the workplace started to gather momentum. I began to engage in hobbies and activities. Family events and eventually marriage and children entered the picture. Inherently, conflict of loyalties became the norm. Burn out was a factor to as vacations and rest to recoup seemed more important in my life. As we know, when it comes to work not all supervisors and employers exhibit compassion and understanding regarding competing attention (to family and personal time) as they work themselves into an early grave or live a lackluster existence.

All said and done how can we balance out the life/work equation?

Before we delve into possible solutions to the life/work balance dilemma a disclaimer is in order. There is no magic bullet answer or no one size fits all solution to everyone's situation. So, let's go on our solution journey.

The first thought that jumps out of my mind is to establish boundaries, perimeters and rules of engagement when it comes to your personal time versus your work time. Of course, how wide or deep your boundaries go depends on your personal obligations at home and your level of ambition at work and among other factors. This article was not meant to catch every single option at your disposal but to kick start your mental gears into motion so that you don't have to wave the white flag in defeat.

Ask yourself, what am I willing to sacrifice? Maybe certain lines of work may not be the best option for a particular point in your life right at this moment. I am not suggesting by any means you cannot have it all as the old axiom goes. Another thought to consider, "can I give this job/personal situation my best effort given my circumstances and the cards dealt or made?

When it comes to duty and responsibility only "you" after much soul-searching can set the stage for expectations. That is what you will or will not accept or tolerate. Generational diversity speaking, if you are on the cusp of retirement, you are at a different level versus a newbie fresh out of college experiencing his or her first job who has yet to prove himself or herself in the workplace. Moreover, more and more employers are operating in a family-type sensitivity zone (allowing parents/caretakers greater latitude when a life/work conflict arises) which was unheard of decades to millennia ago.

Also, let's not forget laws to protect employees such as Family and Medical Leave Act and Paid Family Leave. Albeit forcing the issue of employees sometimes have other than work responsibilities. Another obvious point is to meet with your supervisor about your particular issues so that the employer has a greater understanding for your situation. However, more or less many conflicts are just that just routine conflicts that render you stressed because of the tug-of-war between the life camp and the work camp.

Will missing your child's first spelling bee competition end the world for you? Probably not, but as a loving parent your heart breaks when the call of work duty rears its head at a precious moment in time that will forever be gone escaping a footprint in your memories and camera/recorder of choice. Therefore, you need to decide for yourself what the greatest priorities are at any point in time. As the minister would say, pray and meditate for the right solution.

I would be remised by not mentioning taking regularly planned vacations can help stem the tide of stress and physical exhaustion as you balance work and home life. I remember reading an article years ago in the Automobile Club of America's popular West Ways membership magazine about many people were taking short weekend vacations or staycations around the house or local beach or place of relaxation nearby their residence. These tend to be affordable with minimal costs while reducing the number of sick days and asking your boss for more time off work.

# 4

# Dragon of You

**Meet Your Dragons**

Okay, so you say , "I don't have any dragons. What the heck are you talking about that I have creatures controlling me telling me what to do or not to do. That I need to meet my dragons in order to move forward in a positive direction, is that correct? Any confusion with that rant?"

As I previously indicated in the Introduction, dragons are metaphors for  the obstacles in our lives.

We all have dragons at one point of our lives. Whatever race, sex, ethnicity, color or creed as human beings we can allow life, things or stuff to happen. Call these dragons what you will, they can inhabit us, and take over our spirits. Nevertheless, you must fight it, rebel against its influence it has over you. Closing your eyes won't make them go away. In fact the more fear you have, the more denial you hold onto, the deeper, the larger and the more menacing it grows.

Your dragons are only as strong as you allow them to be. Yes, dragons are scary and intimidating but you have an inner power, a source of energy, will and resiliency to defeat their control over you. Slay your dragons now. Stop procrastinating. Push forward with courage. Are you tired of being tired of whatever it is holding you back from achieving, and from succeeding like you are meant to succeed.

You are never too old, never too young, never too weak, never too lonely and never to broke to change your life. You have the inner strength to defeat these nasty creatures that are smothering you and suffocating your very existence. Don't fall prey as a deer being hunted or stalked by the lion thirsting for blood, planning to slowly savor the meat on your bones until there is nothing remaining of you but a faint uneventful memory.

You have great value as there is only one of you. You are more valuable than all the gold on the planet. Rise up and confront your destiny . It is time to release your dragons. Dragons are very real. You've lost the battle if you think they are myth. That's what they want you to think. They want you to believe that there is no enemy, there is no obstacle and conspiracies to destroy you. Dragons want you to think they are just in your head, nothing real, only a figment of your imagination. Dragons want you to be unfilled, inadequate and desperate, wasting precious time and life as they know time is a scarce resource and commodity, slowly inching away second by second, minute by minute, hour by hour until it's over.

I challenge you to get up and bring the fight to your dragons. Surprise your dragons who are waiting for you to crawl back under your blanket, shaking and quivering until he devours you.

Slay your dragon!

# 5

# Control Over Whom

**We Command our Dragons**

As I write this exciting yet challenging chapter, I am in the process of slaying one of my dragons. The mythical dragons are from what fairytales and legends are made. We see them in a litany of books, films and impartations of wild imaginations from every corner of the globe. Usually these named magical beasts inflict much incomprehensible damage (on a civilization or people) before and/or if they are slain by the hero or protagonist in our story of choice.

Of course, I am not referring to Puff the Magic Dragon, Pete's Dragon or How to Train your Dragon; about the sweet wholesome or nice dragons portrayed in small children's stories. We tend to love those charismatic and very charming dragons. My focal point is those nasty, mean and highly destructive creatures found in movies such as "Reign of Fire" or "The Hobbit: The Desolation of Smaug", a Lord of the Ring prequel. See these fire-breathing dragons established their dominance by setting everything and everyone they could ablaze. Horrifying at minimum to say the least. The heart of their malevolence results in that four-letter word we tough guys or gals deny affect us or control us in any shape, manner, or form, i.e., what we do or say or not.

We all have them, yes ... those dragons somewhere in the inner depths of our souls, minds and very existence, that thing that prevents us from achieving our goals and believing in ourselves. One dragon that takes down a many of us is that fiery dragon we simply call "fear". In my article intro, to what fear I refer? The fear of not writing a good, no, excellent article to my readers. A fear of failing them on some level where the article's value is at question. As my deadline to submit inched closer, I overcame my dragon as I greatly desired to keep my word. Although the sister-dragon of procrastination shackled me for some measure of time.

Let's define the dragon of fear. Fear – to be afraid. To expect or worry about something bad or unpleasant.

These definitions hit us two-fold; in the past and the future avoiding the present reality altogether. After something goes wrong, we reflect on the failure or the lack of achieving our objective which somehow manifest itself into a fear and avoiding yet another opportunity to achieve our goals. In other words, because we fall, we avoid the pain of getting back up and possibly falling again. So, we use the past as a barometer of the future, albeit creating a negative vision of our future. "If you believe you can't then you are correct."

In the end, we stay in a safe place where we are not moving or advancing toward our utopian vision of what our life could be. If we only would try again, but fear or that mean nasty dragon inside of us won't allow us to experience that pain of failure. We short-circuit our future. Therefore, the past is ill-represented and the future we so desperately want is washed away in the sea of lost dreams and lost hope.

As I presented my own fear to you the readers, I was in real-time fighting this psychological and emotionally draining creature attempting to rob me of my future accomplishment of finishing this chapter or more accurately – my goal of helping others overcome their dream-killing dragons.

You see, dragons by definition are inherently designed to stop you or severally delay your goals, your life purpose and your ability to pay it forward. So, this tale about dragons is in so many ways is a story about realizing your goals in life and achieving the achievable or the perceived impossible in the mind (never-going-to-happen) for many people. As I have presented in many of my presentations and workshops over the years millions and billions of people across the globe have missed opportunities or intentionally avoided achieving their dreams or fulfilling their life's work. Many skipped right passed the spirit of accomplishment because they feared that they were not talented enough, not smart enough, or not worthy enough for a cacophony of reasons.

Another way of looking at this is sometimes, more so than not, we do not accept ourselves and our true value in the marketplace, at school or in relationships. Our poor self-perception dictates that we diminish ourselves long before anyone else defines who we are and what we are or not able to accomplish in whatever the setting or station in life now. Yes, undoubtedly, there are external forces that may get in your pathway of success that you cannot control. However, the internal mechanisms within you dictate becoming a master of your own destiny.

What do we do to accomplish our goals and realize our dreams?

To realize your goals, you must defeat the negative chatter in your mind that loudly proclaims you cannot do something. The primary objective is to take your power back. The key to your successful future rightfully belongs in your hands. You are saying sure so simple, easier said than done, yeah right etc. I get it. Defeating a psychological fire breathing dragon aimed to destroy your dreams may not happen overnight or even next week as steps in positive directions do take time. Let me give a simple example of achieving a dream that was not overnight.

Remember when you were a child learning to ride that bicycle you were given for your birthday or Christmas? You wanted to ride your bicycle, didn't you? Sure, you did. But you couldn't because every time you attempted to ride it you initially fell down, right? What did you do next? You got up and picked your bicycle off the ground and tried again. Same results occurred, and you repeated the cycle of failure. That is, until that magical attempt proved successful. You did not give up. Why? Only you know that answer, but I have a few guesses. You wanted to join your friends as they rode to the kingdom of fun leaving you behind.

Or, you were also embarrassed that you were left behind walking or running aside those who achieved their self-serving greatness in riding their bicycles. No matter the reason, you get the point. You did not give up. Those so-called repeated failures were actually giving you the experience on what not do as well what to do in order to ride your bicycle. You learned resiliency and the power of the positive mind reinforced through a never say die attitude of faith and belief in yourself. You may say I still can't ride a bicycle. Well, replace the bicycle example with another achievement where you did not give up and you ultimately achieved your goal or dream.

Slaying your dragons is much more than lessons on just conquering your fears as it is a battle plan on the war against a self-defeating spirit and mindset or fighting for the life you always wanted. Look back on all your achievements to date from kindergarten to adulthood. Most likely in conquering your dragon of choice, whether it be fear, procrastination, or doubt, you pushed forward and did the thing you feared as in the bicycle example.

To delve deeper in the recesses of your mind, ask yourself "how did I overcome and move forward?" Use those answers to help you with your present bucket list or New Year's resolutions you make to yourself every year that go unfilled.

Regardless, of your goals whether it is to lose weight, make more money, unclutter your home or write a song, fight the dragon of fear of failure or procrastination.

My guess is you used principles you learned, mentioned from the bicycle example above or other achieved goals, to accomplish previous bucket list items or wish-lists. I am a firm believer in affirmations and positive quotes. Tell yourself, "Yes I can do this". "Yes, I will fall as I ride the bicycle of life, but I will get back up." Each so-called failure is another opportunity to get closer to achieving the achievable. Optimism is your friend, so embrace looking at situations in a positive light.

What you focus on is what you will attract and bring forth. It starts with your mind – the power of positive energy. Treat focus as a powerful force to be reckoned with. In the hands of a positive mind, it can lead to positive outcomes like realizing your dreams. But in the negative mind that focus can lead to despair, wasting time and bring forth that four-letter word we've been talking about, i.e., "fear". Or more aptly called those dragons of defeat. So, I encourage you to take decisive action immediately by initiating your campaign of achieving your goals by slaying your dragons.

# 6

# Fears Got a Tight Hold

**Dragon**

**of**

**Atychiphobia**

**(Fear of Failure)**

Now, let's directly tackle these dragons. Each and every one of us has our own, homegrown dragon. What do I mean? In reflection, as I grew up, I was terrorized by the dragon of fear which led to other types of dragons. Sometimes, many times Dragons appear to be cute and cuddly, innocent looking and acting if you will.

Haven't you had one of those perfect days where everything was going right until "bam" something happened to challenge or ruin that so-called perfect day? That cute little teddy bear is now a fully charged firing breathing very ugly dragon.

Case in point, you suddenly been assigned a project that is due in 2 or 3 hours that you have no or little idea where to begin or finish, out of your comfort zone.

Or, personally, that loan you applied for which you were originally approved for was reduced or declined and you need the money by end of week. What do we do in these scenarios? We can react emotionally and ride the slide down to the great abyss or we can turn that negative action and emotion to a more rationally influenced mindset.

As you can imagine, there are many dragons waiting to stop you. They will actively pursue you to get you off course. The fact is we may have 1 or 10 dragons or more. Thru self-discovery and soul-searching, you will find them all and then work on eliminating them from your life. They will show themselves. They hide like a thief in the night or invisible to the naked eye like ghosts in the wind.

As you gain awareness, they reveal themselves becoming temporal in the flesh. In this book I'm going to focus on only 3 dragons. The worst dragon is very bad indeed, nearly unstoppable, will stop you from realizing your goals and dreams short-circuiting your life.

## Dragons Everywhere

The Dragon of Fear is the Patriarch or Matriarch of all the other dragons. This one can take you.

out if you allow it. This dragon is the root dragon from where all the other dragons are born. The most dragon difficult to defeat. If you are tired of being tired and you keep an open mind, then you will be victorious.

Look, we are all works in progress, I haven't met anyone that has fully arrived yet. The bottom line is when you fall you can either stay down or rise.

When I was writing this chapter and an article about slaying your dragons, I had some level of apprehension about if I can pull it off and write something that would resonate meaningful with my readers. Although I demonstrated hesitation much of that fear was emotional and just in my head when I gave it much more thought and clarity. You see listening to this dragon can take you to a place where you won't even try or make a good effort to achieve and succeed.

Take me, if I gave in to these dragons, I would not have written my article or this book. I would have avoided calls to present for a seminar or made lame excuses on not presenting on this subject. I would have missed out on blessings and opportunities for sure. Whether we should turn left or turn right or go straight will be based on our confidence or fear or a combination of both. As a people, we will be self-challenged, questioning ourselves if we are on the right track with how we govern our lives and make the decisions we make.

To take action or not to take action. The seeds of doubt are sown partially or wholly from fear. When we make mistakes (and we will) we may unfairly escalate the negative mental chatter from the actual reality of the situation. When we receive constructive feedback, we can take as a positive or take it and drag it through the mud as an abject failure, mentally or internally denigrating our belief in ourselves to be successful. You know the expression of taking it to the extreme. We can take one little thing and blow it up inappropriately outside of reality from what actually happened.

In the workplace, as leaders, when we are faced with underperformance, our own or others it is important to not paint a negative picture of blame or self-destructiveness. If failure is realized and success avoided this can cause fear to want to try again.

The impact is our creative juices are stymied and thinking creatively on an assignment/project will be impaired as a result of our fear of feeling defeated or embarrassed or missing the target yet again. If this happens, we can be left with feeling average or incomplete, not as smart as we originally thought or feeling mediocre thereby minimalizing our contributions to the project, operation, or the team.

Regardless of your profession or position level for the

sake of this chapter I consider you a leader. Therefore, as leaders we must create an environment of creativity, positive reinforcement, nurturing and goal oriented. You can miss out and the ship will sail without you. Not to be religious, you shouldn't have to wait to get your Sushi in heaven. On another note, when the demand to meet your goals are more powerful than your fears you will get courage along the way.

The point is not to wait until you receive courage but do the thing you fear most, and your fear will dissipate, and opportunities will be more in abundant. It's funny when you are looking for something you see more of it. For example, you're looking to purchase a particular car, i.e., Mercedes. For some reason you will see more Mercedes.

You cannot allow yourself to be defined by mistakes or failures. My point is to keep moving forward. Look back only to learn what not to do. There are rarely any overnight successes. What you don't see in others is the many hours, months, or years they spent being a so-called overnight success. The road to achievement is not an easy one. It takes a deep commitment and a long-term outlook. Think turtle versus the hare.

Dragon Names

| | | |
|---|---|---|
| Fear | Procrastination | Dissatisfaction |
| Sadness | Anxiety | Depression |
| Confusion | Low-Esteem | Doubt |
| Anger | Indecisive | Poor Decisions |
| Lack of Focus | Follower | Spendthrift |

As mentioned earlier, emotion is involved when courting or dealing with fear. If we can manage our emotions, we can in turn manage fear. Fear is a noun. It is also a verb meaning we're taking action, and we are in motion.

See fear is something we do. Let's view fear as a noun and verb.

Fear defined:
NOUN

An unpleasant emotion caused by the belief that someone or something is dangerous, likely to cause pain, or a threat. "Fear of increasing unemployment"

VERB

Be afraid of (someone or something) as likely to be dangerous, painful, or threatening.

As you read through this book, I want you to now visualize fear as a fiery breathing quadruped that is capable of not just utter destruction but an ability and the intention of destroying your life. A creature that can outrun you, outthink you and overpower you. There's one catch, what is it you say? All the above is true, except if you allow it to do those things. You mean we have power over fear? Yes, that is correct. In fact, you don't have to fully conquer fear in order to achieve and succeed in your life. Keep reading and you will read the possibilities.

# 7

# Procrastination Waits Forever

**Dragons Patience**

This next dragon is highly destructive and leaves no prisoners. The biggest thing with this insidious dragon is that it doesn't really sneak up behind you or tricks you. It gets you voluntarily with both eyes wide-open. In fact, we actually help this dragon to mess ourselves up. We are partners in its high crimes of a life unfilled and not enjoyed and not achieved.

Procrastination defined:

"The action of delaying or postponing something."

Do you see this definition, "the action of ..."? That's right the action. This surprised me. Definitely educated me. But you say, I thought procrastinating is doing nothing? How can I take action in doing nothing? Procrastination is simple thing to do. To break this concept down I will quote a very famous bear. "By doing nothing we are doing something."

Okay, I will spill the beans. The phrase above is attributed to Winnie the Pooh.

As you may well be aware, there is an impact to procrastination. Here is a list of possibilities:

- Bored
- Stress
- Anxiety
- Health issues
- Insomnia
- Regret
- Embarrassment
- Guilt
- Shame
- Lack of career advancement
- Demotion
- Job loss

What's another way of looking at this thing called procrastination? We can also view it as the struggle with self-control. Wow! I said it. It implies a choice, right? If we manage self-control effectively then we can reduce to eliminate this beast called procrastination. Employee A knows their assignment is due in 5 days.

They know this … undisputed. But they wait, they wait more and wait some more. Perhaps working on a little bit here and there to justify their minimal effort as a great achievement. The other things we may hear or say, I'll do the dishes.

I'll fix it dear, yes, mom my homework isn't due for two more days, I'll do it. I'll go to the dry cleaners tomorrow and on and on. We all get it deep inside, but we'll really get it tomorrow because we got time.

| Procrastination Excuses | Solutions to Procrastination |
| --- | --- |
| I have time. | Don't underestimate your timeline. |
| I work better under pressure. | Know the scope of the project or activity. |
| Before I start or finish, I need … | Understand the impact if not completed in a timely manner. |
| So and so gets the good stuff I get this blank, blank. | Be Flexible |
| I have to be in the mood. | Communicate your concerns with stakeholders or trusted confidants. |

| | |
|---|---|
| I'm being punished. | Modify outlook on life. |
| They don't pay me enough. | "Just do it" |
| I'll do it. | Mind/Eyes wide open |

Please notice that there are many more excuses to not do something or delay action versus engage in solutions. You see for those hardcore procrastinators out there, there will always be a reason and another reason and untold number of excuses to avoid what should be the nonavoidable.

Additional excuses:

- Get off my back
- It must be perfect
- What are they going to do?
- They never trained me
- I feel like a puppet
- Why don't they give this to …?
- I'm too good for this; wasting my time
- Why me?

I will end with this dragon's motto:

"Procrastinators do it tomorrow!"

# 8

# Dissatisfaction Never Joy

**Dragons Spirit**

The third strongest dragon is quite common and more preventable than the other two dragons previously mentioned. Nevertheless, this one hits us primarily at home or the office. This dragon unleashes unhappiness, sadness, frustration, and unleashes the spirit of ungratefulness among other negative related emotions. This dragon causes a significant disruption at home, school, the workplace and wherever there are people. On a very personal note, perhaps you are the carrier of this deceptive dragon as we tend to point the finger at others when it would be most appropriately aimed toward us. Yes, ouch! Straight up.

How so?

First, I will begin with the home. For all you on the cusp of divorce or seriously unhappy with your mate. You probably can read my lips or mouth my words or complete my sentences. Stating the obvious, when a marriage deteriorates it is due to one or both partners being dissatisfied with the other partner typically for a prolonged period of time.

Okay, we know that for a fact. The point is to get to the core of the matter which may never be an agreement. For example, the number one cited reason for disharmony is usually centered around that neutral five letter word that is neither good nor evil, it is money. More so than not it is about the lack of money.

Disclaimer, you can be perfectly single and equally dissatisfied compared to couples. Similarly, you may be experiencing disharmony with your financial situation and future prospects of escaping the hole you have found yourself in.

Back to couples.

Rarer but true, there are instances where a couple has more money than they can count or weigh. The disagreement and fights are about what to do with the money same as a couple on the low end of the spectrum where each dollar counts. You can also find this with lottery winners who recently transcended above their meager living history. The well-to-do folks' problems are just with bigger dollar signs.

The majority of problems are dealing with not earning enough money and being so stressed because of the plethora of bills and expenses that demand immediate attention. Naturally, there are competing demands for your money. The mortgage company wants their cut, the electricity company demands some, the grocery store won't release their food without a cut, the gardener, the barbershop, the car dealer, and the biggest entity with its hand out is the government, local, county, and federal.

Don't forget mommy, daddy and aunt Louise waiting for five years for her money back. Don't get me started if you have children, just empty your wallet or purse. If you dare to have expensive vacations, then God bless you as you struggle with paying the basic necessities.

I am not a minister or licensed therapist. I recommend taking that route if you must in order to move in a positive or productive direction. However, I wrote this book so I will continue to give my commentary.

There is no one size fits all solution. If either you or your mate is dissatisfied there are root causes. Let's lay it all on the table. After all is said and done, you may have married the wrong person or things ran its course, meaning one of you outgrew the other.

That's what happened to me. Sometimes it is no one's fault, things happen. Now for the religious zealots that believe you should stay together no matter what, no matter the reason, God bless you. Some people rather be unhappy until they die. I made the decision to finally be happy at home. Many of you understood what I just said. I discovered very late that there are selfish people out there that shouldn't be married or even dating anyone. These people are not even good to themselves at the end of the day.

Get me started on that movie myth found in Hollywood romantic comedies. 'You complete me". Two halves do not make a whole. That's one of the greatest lies perpetuated throughout the world. If you both aren't wholes then you can bet with almost certainty the dragon of dissatisfaction is waiting behind bush number one, two and he brought a few friends, so bush number three and four are occupied as well.

Some of the issues around money is people did not establish a sound foundation to build a life of comfort. They didn't complete their education or attain the skills necessary in whatever vocation of choice that paid according to their lifestyle of choice. Some had children too early before they got their own lives together. Some inappropriately risked all their money on a venture ill-suited to their ability to sustain the loss of it. Some had bad habits and could not retain a job. I could go on and on about reasons for lack of money.

There are many unfortunate souls that due to no fault of their own they found themselves in a challenging situation. Perhaps a loved one prematurely died or was injured or perhaps someone scammed them of their money. Bad things do happen to good people that deserve much more than they currently possess. I pray for these people. If you have the means, you should help people when possible. I know my plan is to help as many people as humanely and financially as possible.

Much dissatisfaction has to do with making poor decisions. Not just one, but multiple bad choices until the universe speaks and say enough. I am no saint. I know I made outright stupid decisions, one too many and zap, just like an insect zapper. I recovered from bankruptcy, two foreclosures and going broke. A rain of unhappiness showered me for many years.

I briefly know what it feels like to sleep on a cold garage floor or sleep in a very cold car at night. I also know what it is like to survive a suicide attempt which led me to the hospital where certain patients didn't make it that night for similar reasons.

What made the difference was I started making better decisions and not embracing those who are willing and able to do me harm literally and figuratively. My friends, plan for success and reach for the stars and you may just hold one in your hand. The first step is to acknowledge you can do better than the present or the past then do better when you can. Although it isn't as easy as it sounds but it isn't as difficult as your mind fools you either.

To paraphrase the late great Maya Angelou, "When someone shows you who they are believe them; the first time."

In terms of the world of work, things don't get any better for the dissatisfied. Unproductive, lower efficiency and reduced effectiveness, higher absenteeism & tardiness and poor customer service. End result failure to meet goals, expectations, missed milestones, implement policies and low morale.

- The cost in the United States of unhappy employees is very high. $450 to $550 Billion, per Gallup Study/Inc. Magazine
- The Gallup's State of the Global Workplace Report highlights findings from workplaces in 140 countries

The study cited three categories:
Engaged employees Not engaged employees Actively disengaged employees.
Not Engaged/Actively Disengaged

- 87% of workers worldwide and …
- 70% in the U.S. are Not engaged or actively disengaged.
- **Engaged**
- 30% of U.S. are engaged
- 13% U.S. worldwide engaged

Engaged

- 22% higher profitability
- 25% Lower turnover
- 37% Lower absenteeism

- 28% Lower theft
- 48% Fewer staff safety incidents

Nothing but the Facts Are you satisfied with recognition? 24%, yes;/76%, no

- 27% - More opportunities
- 25% - Greater clarity of what/why
- Work harder if better recognized? 77%, yes/23%, no
- 20% - Career opportunities
- 39% No appreciation

Solutions:

- Career Development opportunities
- Challenging work
- Healthy relationships at work
- Coach and mentor
- Praise
- Recognition (public)
- Encourage
- Apply for the right employment opportunity
- Regular Feedback
- Clear objectives
- Hire Talent – the right people for the right jobs
- Nurture employees' skills develop abilities and sense of purpose
- Enhance well-being – body, mind emotion and sense of meaning

- The Hay Group, a global management and consulting firm measured its employee current levels of satisfaction at 10 regional offices. Read stats. Satisfied – 76% NO. Better recognized – 77% YES.
- **Stats from Gallup**

It is important to meet your challenges head-on, facing your challenges directly avoiding the head in the sand as if the issues will go away when taking the head from the sand. Wherever you go the problems go. Face your fears by doing what you fear most. Get professional help if you must as Nike says, just do it.

Do something that will ignite your passion to move forward to meeting your dreams or goals. As Winnie the Pooh says, doing nothing is doing something. That said, with that strategy you are not progressing or achieving.

If you're not achieving something what is the point? Stop kicking that can down the road and start living on purpose. Find your gift. Work your gift. And, share with the world.

As you travel your path learn to do it with a smile and start figuring out what makes you happy then plan to do what brings you joy. Learn from the past, live in the moment and plan for tomorrow. You have only 86, 400 seconds in each day, so use those precious seconds wisely as once a moment in time is gone it is gone forever. Whatever cards you are dealt work with what you got and plan to improve your situation.

# 9

# The Gift

**Would Your Gift to the World be Denied?**

Do you have that special "thing" which you nurtured or practiced over the years, became good at it, something you have the talent or excitement? Or, perhaps, you have yet to discover your gift?

For some of us we knew at a very young age what our gifts are and for others we have been searching for decades. It's possible we suppressed it, forced it in the shadows or locked it away in the closet until that day we find the courage to pursue "it". Before we conquer the dragons in our lives, we must first remove those internal obstacles "that junk" in our lives that is holding us back.

Are you saying Michael Kane before I remove the dragon, i.e., the fear, the low self-esteem, the inferiority-complex, the poor relationships, bad decisions and on and on, I must remove the obstacle of the obstacle which is the "junk" from my life?

Drum roll please … yes. You got it!

Think of it as a 12-step program. What is one of the first things they ask you to do or the expectation after announcing your name? (pause) the new participant declares, "I have this problem or issue in my life that I want to be free of". If you desire success and victory over your life, you must face your giants. Oh no. You mean I not only have to conquer dragons, but I must also confront giants to? Yes. If you never admit to it, it will remain and grow like an infection or virus. You got to be tired of being too tired in to move forward.

**Dragons Take What We Give**

You got to unlock the door of those things that we suppress, those things in our mind that hold us back. Most of us have professional and personal goals and dreams. Not saying incidents or events are just imaginary or fantasy, make believe.

That said, we can exaggerate real issues to the point we are frozen from taking any action. You might say, "if I open that door the boogeyman is going to get me. The Freddie Kruger's or Michael Myers". No, my friends you will get freedom and contentment. Perhaps not overnight but eventually.

No matter who we are, where we are, where we came from, where we've been or where we want to go; over and above all the cultural and race differences; the human race has this in common ... to realize our dreams and life goals, to move forward achieving the dream.

Despite, speaking different languages, wearing different clothes, wearing our hair in various ways, eat different foods we want self-determination, we want to achieve, to prosper, to climb the mountain top. Sounds simple, yes. But not easy by any means.

To identify your gifts, to pursue your gifts and to obtain them and then exercise them, to live the life you always wanted to live is the admirable. Yet, we question ourselves creating a wall of obstacles because of these dragons namely "Fear". In order to gain control, you must find the courage to slay your dragons.

# 10

# Within

**Guess Who's Hiding Inside?**

To move this topic about defeating dragons forward, before we deal with the external miscellaneous dragons you may encounter; the negative situations, drama, or people (family, friends, and not-so-friendlies in our life-frenemies, we first have to deal with ourselves.

Arguably we are the first dragon. That's right, I said it. Do we have any perfect people reading this book today? Sometimes, many times we are the problem or allowing barriers and obstacles holding us back for whatever reasons. Take the mirror out and look.

What do you see?

As you gaze in the mirror looking at yourself. Really look beyond the surface. Focus on your eyes. The eyes are the mirror to the soul, which never lies. The old saying you can fool other people, but you cannot fool yourself.

Indulge me for a moment. Have you heard of the Limbic System? Case in point, you're walking in the crosswalk and a car is speeding at you, it is not stopping. You jump out of the way. Or a snake pops out of nowhere as you hike on a trail. You exhibit fear and run. Was that a reaction or did you wait for a moment to think about it logically?

Let's turn to the intuition. Some people don't subscribe to using the gut, the inner you that communicates all sorts of things. The problem is many people don't listen to it and attempt to use reason only and don't look out for that snake, hiding in the bushes or a rock and get bit by the snake in the hiking story above. The process that gives you the ability to know something directly without thinking. Your inner voice telling you something. It's being aware of 5 senses, i.e., taste, hear, see, smell and touch. Something doesn't feel right (unusual or out of place). Be open to all messages your intuition is communicating.

Many of our Dragons come from emotion, not grounded in facts or reason. Your intuition may be leading you down the correct path. I'm not saying to only use your gut instincts but tap into it to help you make wiser decisions.

You can always validate what you're feeling with the logic centers of the brain and plain old common sense and experience. True, you fell down, true you made a mistake, yes. You don't have to let it define you for the rest of your lives.

# 11

# Tomorrow's Opportunities

**Dragons Feed On Our Dreams**

Anyone here of Rocky Balboa the Italian Stallion?

As you may know, the fictional character Rocky experienced what you and I go through in this thing called life. We all have ups and downs and downs and up. In the series of films showcasing the Italian Stallion, Rocky wasn't a man without fears or other issues. He was plagued with personal challenges like the rest of us during the course of his life.

One thing rocky had was a well-centered belief in himself, and a fighting spirit to persevere to not give up the dream. A winner is not someone that stays on their feet hundred percentage of the time. No, a winner is someone that gets knocked down like Rocky but gets up with the same or more determination he or she started with when they began their journey.

Have you ever been to a boxing match and see what they experience in the ring? Have you been a boxer? You may not have been a Rocky Balboa, but you have been a boxer in spirit. If you didn't grow up with a silver spoon in your mouth, then you likely experienced minor to severe challenges. It's called the boxing match of life.

Yes. Life.

We've all faced the good, bad and the ugly sometime in our lives. Not enjoying life. Amen. Whatever we faced, a financial setback, divorce, unemployment, a sick child, health issues, care of elderly parents and death in family. Did someone lie on you and set you up for failure? Is the thrill gone in your job? As BB King's signature hit song says, "the thrill is gone, the thrill has gone away". Can anyone relate? Yes, life will hit you and knock you down if you live long enough.

My father use to take me once in a while to the great fabulous Forum in Inglewood to see boxing. Although I watched many of boxing matches on television, it was nothing like being there in person. In fact, my father was briefly in the boxing business where he co-sponsored a boxer in East Los Angeles. I soon realized a boxing match can be very brutal. Gladiator stuff. True grit. Those boxers emanated both courage and resolve.

I learned strength of character as each boxer went round after round surviving and not giving up. To be successful and an achiever we have to be that tough. We must teach our children to be tough as well with a dose of compassion for those less fortunate.

Most of us did not start at the top. We worked our way up. However, there comes a time when you think you can't take no more, about to give up. The chatter in your mind shouts, "I can't take one more round in the ring". My friends, that one more punch, that next step, that next 60 seconds could make all the difference in the world between failure to success. Don't give up!

So, what do we do?

Do you know the arcade game Whac A Mole?

Fear is much like this game where when you Whac the mole in the head when he pops out of the hole. You hit him at this hole then the Mole, i.e. (fear) pops its ugly head up from another hole. The game is intended to wear you out and beat you. Defeat you just like this dragon of fear. If you wear out and quit the mole wins/fear wins.

Don't give up! Somehow, we have to get back in the ring, the ring of life.

When you are facing your battles. When you are facing your dragons, when life is not going your way, pick yourself up. When you think you're having a bad day let's talk about the true story of Apollo 13. The crew of the spacecraft Odyssey were on their way on a routine mission to the Moon when equipment malfunctioned, and an explosion crippled the spaceship. Just like life when you have all your plans laid out just so perfectly something can happen to change your original plans.

Murphy's law can kick in at the most inopportune time and derail your carefully laid out plans. This mission of the Apollo 13 was changed from several men travelling to the Moon for research to finding a way back home safely to earth. In other words, if a solution was not discovered soon these men would die in outer space stuck somewhere between the Earth and the Moon.

Eugene Francis "Gene" Kranz was born in Toledo, Ohio. He is a retired NASA flight director and manager. Kranz served as a flight director during the Gemini and Apollo programs and is best known for his role in saving the crew of Apollo 13. Kranz was credited with the famous expression and point of this chapter, "Failure is not an option". It was determined that a damaged coil built inside the oxygen tank sparked during a cryo stir and caused the explosion that crippled the Odyssey.

He is also famous for his trademark flattop hairstyle, and the wearing of vests (waistcoats) of different styles and materials during missions for which he acted as flight director. Kranz has received the Presidential Medal of Freedom.

Needless to say, the astronauts made it home safely as the result of exceptional teamwork and leadership on the ground and on the spaceship.

# 12

# I Didn't Come Here To Lose

**Dragons' Plans**

Lofty chapter title for sure. Perhaps somewhat arrogant. Not settling on plan B. The mantra screams, "Plan A all the way!"

"We will win, no exceptions." We have won before winning because we are the best." Okay, a bit on the aggressive side. The above statements are clearly from someone that wants to win at something. No holds bar and take no prisoners. Beyond the topical, think about it deeper for a moment hopefully without being dismissive as a lost braggadocios cause.

A side bar for a moment. I got the idea for the title of this chapter from my father. More accurately, from his baseball style hat which had the title inscribed on it. I only have a vague memory of this hat many years ago as my father died almost 12 years ago. Reflecting on my dad, he taught me success is it not a bad thing but an admirable goal which means different things to different people.

Let's put it in a sports team perspective. Visualize that you're at a football or basketball game overhearing (the coach to his players) for the team you came to see and paid $200 stretching your budget in the process. Gentler, "I didn't come here to lose, and you didn't come here to lose, did you?" "I said, did you?"

Now the words don't seem as harsh or inappropriate. You see we tend to make exceptions depending on the context. These statements are representations of the power of positive thinking. Take the above comments outside of a game or sport then people may accuse you of being inappropriate or only caring about the winning and not the self-development or cooperative side. Values will be assumed to be missing if you shout victory too loudly. There is some merit in viewing excessive optimism as arrogant.

I'm not one of those people that exudes excessive pollyannish approaches to life. I do believe affirmations have a place in reinforcing good thoughts. However, faith without works is dead. My viewpoint is that happy energy must be backed up by action and forward thrust motion. I do believe good or useful habits do begin in the mind and spirit.

But if they do not manifest in the real world all you have

are those thoughts leading you on the road to nowhere at least in the physical realm. You will not benefit in any real sense of satisfaction, monetarily, health wise, relationships or various forms of accomplishments.

Back to my sports analogy. When you were in school did you ever play in a sport? You and your teammates worked hard every school day and probably on the weekends my guess. This was extracurricular activity, so you still had to attend classes and do homework. Of course, chores at home didn't evaporate because your school life was tough.

My point is you engaged in all the rituals of succeeding in terms of academics and the rigors of sports because you wanted to win. You wanted to be a conqueror a king or queen, on the mountain top. Your intentions were to be the best. As you played your sport you wanted your team to score the highest points than your opponent and be declared the victor, plain and simple.

For those students that didn't play in a sport, I don't want to exclude you. If you were in the band or academic decathlon or chess club, you wanted the same thing. You as well worked hard, practicing, rehearsing, and experiencing late nights honing your craft, hobby, or activity. You to faced challenges, frustration, and the euphoria of victory. You loved the feeling of accomplishment and to be recognized for those achievements. Perhaps you love the adulation of the crowds and attendees, it made you feel great inside and outside. You felt needed and joyful. It was nice to earn awards, trophies and attention. Whether you were accomplished in school at whatever grade level for academics or talent you were and are special. If you simply graduated performing at the best of your ability you are accomplished and did more than many people. Therefore, you should be congratulated.

Now that you are an adult that feeling, and expectation of winning did not suddenly vanish. My bet is if you achieved fifth place it's not the same feeling as taking home the gold despite moving past your youth. The desire is great to get the trophy in your hand. Although life challenges can get in our way for sure. We sometimes find ourselves burned-out lost in a sea of mediocrity barely holding on rather freely swimming in the sea of excellence.

Whatever your vocation, skill, or degree you are still that winner you were back in the day. Regardless of if you work in a blue collar or white-collar job you still can work hard and navigate your ascension up the proverbial ladder. You may have to change jobs, careers or start your own business along the way, but you have it in you to win that gold medal.

Your achievements may not necessarily be what you envisioned them to be but welcome any degree of success. Some moments in your life are mere steppingstones for something much greater yet to happen in your life. Perhaps not today per se but down the road.

Don't take any learning opportunity for granted. I make an effort to learn from everyone I meet. You say, yeah right, sure you do? I do. I make a point to learn and use experience from working with angels down to the devils in life. I worked for one challenging soul who made it his daily routine to disseminate his evil and wickedness to others including your truly.

It was a living hell working for that creep. His poor inexcusable behavior that was sanctioned by higher level executives by doing nothing, taught me and reinforced what great leadership really looked like. You see people teach what you should do but also what you should not do. The universe will take care of the good, the bad and the ugly, just in different ways. Some call it Karma and others you reap what you sow. Amen.

When you see someone doing something smart that would benefit you if you moved in that direction then emulate that behavior. The opposite is true if you see stupid, your lesson for that is don't do stupid but run as fast as you can. Either way, you learn. As they say, it will be either a blessing or lesson. Just keep moving forward.

# 13

# The Dr Doesn't Live Here Anymore

**Dragon**

**of**

**Hypochondria**

**(Fear of being Sick)**

An apple a day keeps the doctor away. A clichéd phrase from my childhood. It's a bit corny but has merit in its fundamental meaning.

If we break it down, we have this formula:
An Apple = eating healthy

1. A Day = a positive habit of taking care of your precious body

2. Keeps the doctor away = you are avoiding illness thereby avoiding seeing a doctor

The road to attaining and maintaining good health starts with that simple phrase of an apple a day keeping the doctor away. Your health plan does not have to include apples, but it wouldn't hurt can only help. This chapter is not solely about eating apples but let's explore apples for a moment. Apples will serve as a place holder for any healthy food you are including on your road to optimum health.

Apples are low in calories and carbs. Apples contain an abundance of important nutrients such as vitamins, fiber, minerals, and antioxidants. Apples may reduce your chances for heart disease, reduce blood pressure & cholesterol, strokes, and inflammation. It may even help you avoid certain cancers such as lung cancer and colorectal cancer.

Wow!

You mean apples can help me maintain good health? Absolutely my friends. Again, this is not a story about just apples but of you becoming and staying physically fit. My goal is to cause an insurrection against unhealthy eating habits. My long-range mission is to persuade you to join my revolt toward living a life free from disease, chronic ailments, and decreased life span.

Healthy habits include eating nutritious foods such as, my apologies, "apples" and drinking lots of water. I promise the

Apple industry is not giving me kickbacks for this endorsement. Truth be told, growing up I resisted as best I could voluntarily eating many healthy foods. But in my day, there was swift punishment for disobedience. Resistance was futile to borrow that line from the Borg for those Star Trek Generations and Voyager fans. If we didn't eat our vegetables and fruit, then consequences were coming. Most definitely desert such as cake or cookies were not in our future as well as any fun time.

The more desirable foods from a child or teenager 's viewpoint came with conditions and costs. So, I ate those green vegetables, melons, plumbs, apples, oranges and more than I can remember. As a kid the CC diet was the norm, the secret norm.

Okay, I know you are curious about the CC diet. CC meaning the cookie and candy diet. I was naively proud for those five or six cavities. We made the dentists happy enabling the purchase of mansions, BMWs, Mercedes Benz and ivy league educations for their children.

Reducing your sugar intake will help your health a thousand-fold if not more. As a child throughout adulthood, I had been addicted to sugar. Oh, I could eat anything sugary at any time of the day. Remember those cubes you would drop in your coffee? It got so bad I was eating sugar cubes at my work cubicle. Moreover, I had coffee with my sugar, quite literally. Ten cubes please were my motto.

Well, they dropped in my mouth, one, two, three so forth. Now a days, there are plenty of sugar substitutes to choose from and avoid the processed sugar. Did you know sugar can cause inflammation? Yes, that's right, eating processed sugar can cause an inflammatory response in the body. Not good if you already suffer from inflammation. You might as well confess at least to yourself what habit you need to eliminate or moderate. That Carly Simon song, "Haven't Got Time for the Pain", rings in my ears.

Most people change their behavior until they are too tired of being tired of whatever the issue is. The biggest problem with kicking the can down the road is your issues may grow exponentially be then causing you more problems, more time and more money to fix.

To draw an analogy, eating excessive sugar is akin to throwing gasoline in a burning building. The building in this case is your body. Don't be a food arsonist, not a good thing for sure. On the flip side there are foods that can reduce inflammation quite naturally.

I will list these Inflammation prevention lifesavers:

1. Legumes
2. Omega-3
3. Omega-6
4. Flaxseeds
5. Fresh fruits
6. Nuts

7. Seeds
8. Whole grains
9. Green leafy vegetables
10. Low-fat dairy

I encourage you to do your research of these and much more. I'm only giving you a primer not a detailed lesson plan.

Water is a Godsend. Drinking this very plentiful basic drink can save and extend your life. Figuratively speaking if you don't believe me try going without it for a couple of days. Please don't do that because there are harsh consequences for failing to drink sufficient water. Water is the gift of life. It keeps our organs operational and gives us energy. Do your own research on drinking this natural drink for optimal health. Nevertheless, I will give you some facts about the clear liquid.

Did you know that your body is composed of 60% water? The body has an array of fluids that water will help balance. The functions of these bodily fluids are saliva creation, maintenance of body temperature, absorption, digestion, and circulation.

Here's a list of benefits from drinking water:

1. Reducing risk of heart attacks and strokes
2. Low blood pressure
3. Lowers Cholesterol
4. Headache prevention
5. Lubricated joints

6. Energy boost
7. Cancer prevention
8. Increased metabolism
9. Reduces water Retention (swollen feet, legs and hands)
10. Eliminates toxins from blood
11. Healthier skin
12. Improved eye health
13. Increased serotonin (depression prevention)
14. Better digestion
15. Sleep improvement (melatonin- regulates sleep pattern)

Okay, I mentioned eating healthy, reducing sugar, and drinking water. The final component is exercise. Yes, you must exercise to round out your road to health plan. You don't need a fancy gym membership, although they can get you out of the house and inspire you to excel in your effort to lose weight, stay fit and eat sensibly.

However, there are numerous exercise you can do right in the comfort of your home such as stretching, yoga and calisthenics. Exercise can increase your endurance, improve your cardiovascular function, and enhance your metabolic rate helping you to burn fat more efficiently. Plus, you can purchase a home gym or inexpensive treadmill, which can help you mimic walking or running outdoors.

In addition to the above, there are many more things you can do as you travel on your road to good health. In short, making sure you get sufficient sleep, at least eight hours. I know this is always not possible because of the busy lives we all live. But you see remarkable improvement in your energy levels physically and emotionally.

Other beneficial foods include other foods like garlic, bananas, sweet potatoes, tomatoes, eggs, poultry, beans, salmon, fatty fish and more. You'll find eating the following leafy greens are not just tasty but beneficial to optimal health: kale, spinach, bok choy, dark lettuces are loaded with folate, iron, magnesium and antioxidants. Eating some of these foods may also reduce type 2 diabetes as well.

The food mentioned in this chapter will provide you needed protein, beta-carotene, vitamin C and E, potassium, fiber, nutrients and healthy fats. Remember to lower your sodium intake. This will help reduce the risk of several diseases and unhealthy conditions.

Again, I encourage you to read up and do your research on maintaining a healthy body and live a much more rewarding life. I wish you well on your road to good health.

# 14

## The Magic Wand

**Dragon Of
Rhabdophobia
(Fear of Magic)**

Let's have fun with this chapter.

Although the character in this chapter is written as a male gender this works the same for the female persuasion as well, no bias intended. That said, let's jump in this story.

Imagine with me that one day as you take a stroll through your local park on a mission to improve your health, you come across this weird looking stick about a foot long. You pass it by when your curiosity as gotten the best of you. You hesitantly pick up the stick. You wave it around pretending to be a kid again. You mutter some words as you wave the odd-looking stick.

As you continue strolling leaving the park onto a residential neighborhood, you noticed your neighborhood doesn't look the same anymore. The architecture reminds you of a time long ago. The houses are painted different colors, what was brown is blue and what was blue is white and so forth. The cars are models you haven't seen in decades, since you were about twelve years old. Fellow strollers are decked in attire you've seen in period films, dated for sure.

You're thinking to yourself that you lost your mind, questioning your sanity. What happened, you mumble to yourself. "Is there a costume party nearby?", you blurted under your breath. You think those sci-fi shows aren't so unbelievable now. The Twilight Zone here we come!

As you continue your stroll in absolute bewilderment, a few young boys cross your path. You recognize an old friend that you haven't seen in many, many years. You said to yourself, "it couldn't be him". "How?"

Your old friend appears to be 12 or 13 years old.

Your mind is telling you to rationalize what is happening. However, your heart and intuition tell you it's got to be him as you recall with certainty the peculiar scar on his right check that you helped put there playing football. Suddenly, you blurt out "Johnny is that you?" 'Do I know you mister?' The boy retorts back. You are motionless, frozen in time wondering what to say next. The boys nervously play out this awkward scene. Instead of writing this off as a bad day-dream and avoid being labeled a pervert, you hesitantly state, "Are you Johnny Roberts?" Then you turn to another boy recognizing him, Blinky? I know all of you. Franky …don't you remember, I'm … I'm …

Before you force your thoughts out one of the boy's shouts, "he's a weirdo we shouldn't talk to strangers." Another boy proclaims, "crazy old man." They take off running. "No, don't go. Come back. I'm Stevie … I'm Stevie Smith."

Somehow you have travelled back in time. You focus on the wand with a puzzled expression reflecting on what just happened. Tearfully, you said, "I want to go home", you mumble. Your face mirrors your scared and fuzzy thoughts. You check the time on your wristwatch. You become dizzy and your head starts spinning until you faint. Moments later, you hear a man on the street, "mister you, okay?" "Wake up, you need a Dr.?" Although a bit groggy you realize you traveled back to your time. You stare at the older gentleman who appears to be similar in age as if he's familiar. The man states, "you want me to call someone?" You let the man help you up and you continue back home, knowing that the older man was Johnny Roberts. This time you kept your thoughts to yourself not wanting to scare your old friend off for a second time. You said, "what was I thinking? Wishing to go back, start my life over again, how stupid." You berate yourself for a few minutes.

Okay, fantasy time is over. What's the point of the story you say?

The takeaway is you let the past stay in the past.

Haven't you ever caught yourself reminiscing of the good old days? Dreaming if you had another chance in life to do a few years over again. How about an entire lifetime do over, would you? Many people would run for the chance to re-live their time on this earth but avoid the not so good times and change things. You're thinking life would be better the second go-around. Like a beauty makeover, would you accept a life makeover?

Some of you are probably saying, "I love my life. I wouldn't change a thing." Oh really? We covered some of the items in another chapter. However, I'm doing my best to drive this very simple point home to those willing to at least consider alternatives to thinking that got them into trouble in the first place.

Excuse my pessimism and doubting the validity of that mindset. Things to reconsider to have another chance to do right include but not limited to: marrying the right person, make better "real" friends, the career of your dreams, i.e., purpose, listening and accepting objective wise counsel, affordable vehicle that won't cause you to lose sleep or get 3 to 4 jobs to pay the monthly payment on time, buying the right size home avoiding bankruptcy, and finally, seizing the opportunity that slipped through your fingers losing a baby fortune or a huge Amazon type fortune. I can go on, but I will stop, point made.

But you wouldn't change a thing, right?

Let's face it, most of us earthlings have some measure of regrets and sorrow over something. Or at least something we were supposed to do but didn't for whatever reason. And if we had a real magic wand, we would swish it around and replay that pivotal moment in time and alter our lives for the better. That's my opinion on the majority.

Now, for the extremist that may say you weak minded folk need to get over it and deal with the now, the present. Stop hating your lives and be grateful. There is some level of truth in those statements. However, personally, I don't hate my life. I love it not all of it but enough of it. Those things I don't presently like I am taking action to improve or change it if possible. I am not suggesting that you become a miserable ingrate hating your life. Moreover, I'm not advocating living in the past wasting precious present seconds, minutes, hours, or days.

What I am saying is to learn from the past but even more so, extract those things from your past that you always wanted to do or rewrite and reconciling your past with your present. Instead of oppressing sad or painful memories of what should or shouldn't have happened to focus on moving forward. A good exercise is to write those good experiences and memories on a separate piece of paper from the bad and ugly.

Next write on another piece of paper those things that you want to do and still may be realistically able to do one day. Essentially, these future things are what we call your bucket or wish list. Yes, those things we want to do before we die.

When we were small children and perhaps teenagers, we dreamt big and wide. Dreams that popped up uncontrollably regardless of if we were sleeping or daydreaming of the possibilities. It's funny when we're young we are unstoppable. Then we grow up then suddenly all these limitations rear their ugly heads telling us we cannot do these things in our dreams. In many instances one of those impossible dreams was our purpose and our direction.

- So, what did you not get to do in the previous chapters of your life?
- What burns you, those deep desires that has resurfaced in the corners of your mind?
- What did you abandon that you gave up for dead?

Now whatever it is you may have an opportunity to make it happen. I recommend jotting your ideas down, brainstorming regardless of how stupid they sound. No matter how impossible it may seem, write those ideas down .... Now!

At some point, you need to select one idea, your biggest and most promising idea. Next, create an action plan of potential pathways you can take to make this idea come true. You probably may have to do a lot of research and investigation. I didn't say this would be easy or possible. You will have to devise a plan to establish the time and money to make this thing happen. Visualize that you really do have a magic wand, do the Harry Potter thing.

My goal is to help stoke your imagination and creativity, to reignite your zeal for life and your future. Back to those pieces of paper that listed the bad and ugly of your past. Ball it up, tear it up and purge it from existence. Easier said and done for sure.

Don't dwell in the past just reflect on it so that living in the present and planning for the future is not only tolerable but most rewarding. You see the endgame here is contentment, living in joy and realizing an abundance of accomplishments. It's great if you receive support from family and close friends. Support could mean emotional, psychological, prayer and some other type of assistance other than money. If you're not receiving these things, then reach out and air your concerns with a confidant.

You may need to contact a licensed counselor or minister. Do your best to press on with your goals with or without full support, within reason of course. Unfortunately, magic wands don't really exist except in fictional stories along with unicorns, fairies, and Pegasus.

I am not advocating disregarding and abandoning those closes to you in your quest. What I'm saying is life is tenable and we don't know how long we will be on this earth. That said, push on what you need to do while you can still have an opportunity to do it. Using your mythical magic wand is ultimately a life changer which will require a transition period.

The key is to keep moving forward until you reach your destination. Don't walk this journey alone seek personal and professional assistance.

# 15

# Do It my Way

**Dragon of Kakorrahaphobia (Rejection)**

As you walk through life there will be occasions that you will want to persuade others to your line of thinking, chart your own course or defend your point of view. You may have read books, many books in fact on the subject. There is no shortage of advice on this topic. When I hear the phrase "my way" a phenomenally successful entertainer comes to mind as you may be familiar.

The imitable Mr. Frank Sinatra. Also aptly called the "the Chairman of the Board". He sure lived a life his way. if we can all be as fortunate and blessed. I encourage you to listen to the song as he brilliantly and eloquently belts out, he did it his way.

You might say you don't have to persuade anyone on anything because you don't do sales. You think so?

Let me digress and attempt to persuade. Every year if not every month or every day you are persuading someone on something either directly or indirectly, consciously, or subconsciously. Let's cut to the chase. Anyone in a serious relationship? My guess is you persuade your significant other daily or at least regularly. I will be your proxy and raise my hand for your silent agreement.

Anyone with children ranging from toddlers to young adults can raise their hands as well. Yes, you may be tough but even the greatest of authoritarians have a down moment of waving the flag of defeat (call it avoidance) or diplomatically welcoming some level of peace with young children or those in-between to young adult when those disagreements pop up.

The next group is if you are an employee working for the" boss" or affectionately called the man. Have you ever vied for a promotion or competed for a special assignment or patiently waited for acknowledgement or opportunity?

If you are upwardly mobile focused, then gaining favor, diplomacy and impressing your viewpoint is in your blood and strategy in reaching the promised land of elevated rank, position and income. As you might know, the workplace can be fraught with hazards and perils when working with and for others. It can be a place full of politicking, brownnosing, and backstabbing as co-workers engage in frontrunning.

Working hard is not the only ingredient and not solely

good enough in the race for survival or promotability in today's workforce. In order to be a viable candidate on the obstacle course of career longevity and success one must be a proactive persuasive navigator and have someone backing you. As all is not equal by any measure.

In essence, you must have engaged in persuasive activities to make it as far as you have in terms of where you stand at this present moment in time.

You say you're self-employed answering to no one because you are the boss or the top cheese. You think so? Do you have any employees or investors? Okay, no and no. Do you have to answer to local, state and federal regulators on any matter, like taxes, fires safety or building codes?

Obviously if you have employees or investors, you know what it takes to deal with both groups. Surely, there were disagreements or different expectations at some point along the way of the relationship. Then raise your hand and move on.

Did you ever buy a product or service and not accept the first price the nice salesman blurted at you? Think car and home. Not much debate here. If you are in a sales position congratulations as you already have a head start to convincing others that your proposal or position is in their best interest. You ever hear the expression, "what's in it for me" or WIFM for short? Regardless if you did or not you already practiced it.

The point of my rant or diatribe of persuading you was to illustrate that you already have the innate ability to move people to your way of thinking. Perhaps you just need refinement and direction to be consistent and draw upon certain proven strategies. One skillset that will help you is to develop your public speaking ability. It is widely known that those who are great at speaking gain favor and demonstrate their potential for moving up in their organization or prospering in their business.

There are numerous books on the subject on how to present your topic of interest to groups of people. Amazon and Barnes & Noble are great resources for books for beginners or more seasoned speakers. If you want to save money, you may pay a trip to your nearest library.

Another major form of communication that will help garner trust in your position or proposal is to master writing excellent sales, marketing, or business letters. Many if not most charitable organizations raise funds through convincing others that their organization is most worthy of your donations. Organizations such as the United Way, the Salvation Army, Goodwill and the Los Angeles Mission are good examples of persuasively requesting donated good or funds through written communications. There are many other excellent organizations that are too numerous to mention. But you get the idea.

Although this chapter and book is not a full description or manuscript on how to be persuasive, it will hopefully spark a fire in you to develop the essentials skills concerning the topic. The art of persuasion involves many moving parts. In reference to my experience, understanding what exactly you want, or need would be the priority. Research will be your friend when making your case.

Once you identified the why and why nots, you should write down all the pros and cons you can think of in favor and its oppositions. To accomplish this task, simply take a piece of paper and draw a vertical line labeling the left-side pros and the right-side cons. This is not to suggest you must back down if your list on the con side is longer than the pros. This exercise is to prepare you to overcome potential objections when presenting to your intended audience. Supporting your vision with facts and statistics never hurts but supports your position and expertise on the subject matter.

Practice your speech presenting your case intelligently and authoritatively, until you hone your presentation down. You want to speak with passion and depth. Writing a detailed outline and thesis statement will prepare you adequately for presenting your case and for a potential battle. Additionally, I would run your arguments past a trusted friend or mentor.

Be careful who you share your ideas with, not to be paranoid, but to ensure your planning is not circumvented, thwarted by a blabber mouth or back stabber. Remember that famous O'Jays song, Backstabbers? "They smilin' in your face all the time they want to take your place the back stabbers".

I may write a book one day on all the backstabbers that I experienced during my life, a tell all book.

Now, go for it.

# 16

# Vision

**Dragon Of Decidophobia (Making Decisions)**

To live a purposeful and successful life it is important that we have a clear understanding of whom we are, where we envision ourselves one year, five years or ten years from today. Do we have a crystal ball? Most likely not. However, to arrive at any destination requires a road map. It also requires a plan to get us there.

Regardless of your current station in life, you can arrive at your intended destination sooner than later. Yes, that's absolutely correct. With a viable plan of action anything is possible. Let's take a step back for a moment, you can be an employee, a small business owner, a CEO of a large company, a homemaker, a student, a manager, or retiree and still feel unsatisfied and unhappy. It's not about the stuff you accumulate but the quality of life which is defined by you. The endgame is you can do something about it. It meaning, your fulfillment and happiness.

How?

Discovering a clear vision, is your catalyst for achieving your goals and exceeding your wildest expectations. Your heart's desire may be what is missing from even realizing extraordinary success in your current field. Without clarity of direction, we may flounder traveling paths unintended wasting precious time. Going down the wrong path is a penalty of an unfocused vision. This is not just about vocation and working the right job or career. This is about destiny and where your mind, body and spirit scream out for you to do and to be.

In reflecting, my belief is that many off us lose focus somewhere in childhood, perhaps on the precipice of high school, let's say at the ripe old age of 14 years. There's no science in this arbitrary number. We all have our own year in which confusion and lack of confidence kicks in for us. Your number could very-well be 12 or 13 or 17 or later in life. In many of my workshops and motivational speeches I have shared that when we were little kids, we did not hesitate what our vocation or dream would be.

Our picture was very clear on what we're planning to do with our professional lives. On the personal front we did not waiver there either. We were comfortable in our shoes so to speak. As we were asked the following question growing up the images or thoughts sprang immediately to our vocal cords, "Johnny what to you want to be when you grow up?" A policeman. This turned into a fireman, astronaut or teacher depending what day you asked the question. The point is we had a strong conviction with a line drawn in the sand and nothing could change our decision. That is until we changed our minds or worse allowing others in our minds watching our dreams blow up or disintegrate.

If part of us could never grow up most of us would be better off. It something about becoming an adult. We seem to lose sight of what makes us happy and content. As mentioned, we allow others to get in our head and start altering those things most important to us. This is not saying imparting wisdom into someone is a bad thing. It is vital that we coach, mentor our children and youth.

However, it is another thing exerting your superior will on an impressionable upcoming adult leading him or her down a path that is forced or pushed.

Back to my thoughts about not growing up. When we grow up, we tend to lose that spark that is birthed in our inner self, i.e., the spirit. In our childhood, we have a magic that propels us to greater thoughts about the possibilities that are open to us, free to believe the unbelievable. To quote the immortal Peter Pan, "I'll never grow up". Peter Pan was written by Sir James Matthew Barrie, aka, J.M. Barrie. The successful nineteenth century Scottish novelist and playwright who was inspired by the Llewelyn Davies boys in London, England. Peter was magical and ageless, who simply did not want to grow up and miss out on life.

He even knew it was something lacking, something wonderful that escaped adults that originated in their childhood that they had somehow lost growing up. Peter was determined that it would not happen to him as he sought a life of adventure.

No, I'm not saying to quit your job and live out the fantasy long forgotten. I'm not saying you should stay or tolerate your existence either. You should be mindful not to abandon your commitments and priorities. My goal is to stir up that inner child in you to regain that spark so you may live in a joyous and happy state. You need to decide what that means to you. I would be remiss in not mentioning my older brother Maurice S. Kane Jr. Case in point, from a young age he just knew he wanted to be an attorney. He was a rare breed that narrowed in on his future vocation sooner than later.

My brother was determined and passionate steadfastly pursing his dream, making sure each step he took moved him closer to his goal or dream. Not only did my brother identify the exact vocation he was to pursue, but he also selected the vehicles to take him there. The University of Southern California and Harvard Law School.

I am not name-dropping or getting paid to mention these top educational institutions, I am pointing out that my brother had a plan of action and that he made our family divinely proud. Most of us wished we were that clear with our vision for our lives and the path to travel in order to realize it.

Now take me, as a child I knew I wanted to be manager or leader over something. The problem was I didn't exactly know what I wanted to manage nor how I was going to get there. I made sure my grades were good enough to maintain some good choices, but I did not do my best all the time, like a roller coaster of commitment up and down toward the pursuit of my objective.

When I graduated high school, I had A's, B's and those occasional C's, not bad but just not my best because my vision was still formulating, and indecisiveness had overwhelmed by cerebral cortex. Needless to say, doubt and low self-esteem were my pain points. I agonized over what to do with my life. In the interim, I had good jobs and challenging ones along the way. Notice I never said all were well paying but good. Good to me was meaningful, rewarding and felt like I mattered. Regardless of good or bad I learned and grew from the experiences. Nevertheless, I was blessed every step of my journey.

It is natural to vacillate while we are finalizing our vision, while we are considering all our options. Seeing clearly takes time and patience. But equally important it takes consistent action. Like Peter Pan, you need to tap into your heart and spirit, not just your mind. Logic is good and may take you far, but insufficient regarding matters of the heart and purpose.

Once you identify your gifts, talents and interests then marry them with your cause then you are able to embark on your vision journey. A cause is what stirs you up inside. That thing that makes you get up early and go to sleep late in the night.

It's the "it" that drives your ambition and that burns the fires of desire. This vision journey is akin to Dorothy, Scarecrow, Tin Man and the Cowardly Lion on their sojourn to the Land of OZ to meet the great Wizard. You see these four fictional characters risked life and limb hoping and wishing the Wizard will grant them their heart desires, i.e., their goals and dreams.

There were obstacles for sure between the start of their journey to the end of it. The Wicked Witch of the West had other plans for them. Naturally, wicked plans that meant utter doom for the quartet. Cursed Poppy fields, flying scary monkeys and terrifying soldiers and much more were tools to stop them from realizing their destiny.

You to will face the bad and ugly on your road as you implement your vision. Like our Wizard of OZ heroes, you must face your fears, hostile combatants, and life challenges. Much can be learned from these characters. There will always be dark forces in the world wanting, wishing, and facilitating your failures. By forces I mean people and situations and things totally out of your control.

Despite the next obstacle in their path, Dorothy and crew

continued regardless of their negative feelings at the time. They took the left foot and then the right foot and kept going until they reached their destination. The same is true for you. You must not give in to lack of courage but press through until the courage replaces the fear.

Were Dorothy and crew scared? Absolutely. Were people or creatures trying to hurt them and stop them? Absolutely. Did they have doubts and fears? Absolutely. Did isolation in an unknown world block and detour them from their road? Absolutely. Did they experience failure? Absolutely.

I believe the greater your vision, the greater the enemy will be to attempt to stop you. In reference to stories in books, TV, or film, is the antagonists stronger or weaker than the protagonists? Typically, the bad guy is bigger, smarter, and more intimidating than the good guy. At least initially, then as the story unfolds and runs its course, the roles reverse, and the hero whips the villain and the goons in the end. You see the hero fails and fails and is discouraged and, in some cases, nearly destroyed on his/her journey.

There is no road free from pitfalls and challenges. Many roads are designed to prevent you from reaching your destiny or purpose. What happens to the hero? The hero grows from the inside and out. The hero develops character and inner strength as the fiery darts zoom at her doing their best to take her down.

In many of non-fictional and fictional stories, the hero

does get taken down. But as the sun arises so does the hero in continuing or even struggling to finish the vision journey. The hero may get bruised, beat up and broken and experiences out right failure, regardless the hero finds inner strength to persevere.

Like our fictional hero, we all have already experienced some type of loss, some pain and suffering in the real world. What do we do? We process the loss, grieve, cope as best we can and somehow, we deal with it. At some point the good days outnumber the bad days. Setbacks in life will happen due to no fault of our own. In many instances or points in time as we walk through life, situations will happen that are totally out of our control. Yes, we will beat ourselves up, losing sleep and cursing our own existence. No matter how much we take responsibility the fact is we could not change the course of whatever negative that happened.

I am sure you have watched movies or television shows where a character travels back in time to prevent a catastrophe from happening. Each time they go back they alter history but something bad still occurs, perhaps even worse than the original circumstance.

Now let's look at the flipside. On the other hand, some opportunities slip through our grasps because we made the wrong decision although the voice of wisdom was yelling, screaming, and kicking us to alter course.

I know some people will take these comments to the

extreme and never accept responsibility. These people always blame others for their own shortcomings. I know from experience as I lived many years with that heavy anchor.

Failure is part of life and so is making poor decisions. If you act as if you don't participate in unwise decisions or experience problems because of your own actions, then you are the mirror of perfection and you must have disciples. Arrogance can come back to haunt you.

For instance, have you ever been in a disastrous relationship? To be honest, your vision instincts kicked in at some point or deep reflection on something that occurred, and you experienced an omen to alter course on this relationship, perhaps to abandon it altogether. You continued the relationship. Then another forewarning came your way and you made additional excuses and you dismissed the clarity that you possessed and continued going down the wrong path. You continued the relationship despite a meteor of evidence slamming into your life, dragging you down. Other in your face moments could be a bad business deal that was wrong from the start and your intuition warned you. Or losing most of your money to a money losing scheme that never had a chance to get off the ground because it was transparently foolish. I can go on and on you get the idea.

Most of us have been down the bad roads mentioned above. To err is human; to forgive is divine. In these cases, you must forgive yourself and stop blaming yourself forging a perpetual unforgiving hell. Wherever you are, whatever your circumstances you can still pursue your vision journey.

It's never over until you say it is over. The point is live your vision and move forward. The only place you can really start is from where you stand today. Today, not yesterday and certainly not tomorrow. Yesterday is in the history books and tomorrow should be worried about tomorrow, although planning for the future in an optimistic way can be a good thing.

The key to working your vision journey is to start making good decisions. At least make more good ones than bad decisions, a net plus versus minus. Don't cheat yourself from a rewarding future by being short sided.

You should be you and not an imitation of someone else. Be true to thyself. It's okay to mimic or borrow good and prudent behaviors from someone you admire and that has achieved a degree of success.

There is commonality of successful people." The 7 Habits of Highly Effective People', a phenomenal book by Stephen R. Covey. He identified similar habits of successful people. The book pointed you in the direction of adopting these same habits and you to will be successful at least goes the premise. There is a high degree of truth in implementing behaviors and actions of others that stand where we want to stand. As long as you are being you in the process.

Remember that timeless song by Johnny Nash, "I can See Clearly Now?". This song should be our anthem as to where we are headed. "I can see clearly now the rain is gone. I can see all the obstacles in my way. Gone are the dark days that had me blind. It's going to be a bright sun- shiny day."

The above are the lyrics of optimism, clarity and purpose. For you to move toward your vision you must work on slaying your dragons and conquer your giants. I encourage you to crawl or run to your promised land.

You must take action as doing nothing is not a goal or achievement. Making changes in your life is not easy. Even those that you know will benefit you.

As the popular Nike commercial said, "just do it". Yes, easier said than done. The point is to start your vision journey. If you wait until you are totally confident it may be too late.

Opportunities will pass you so fast you may not even recognize them. You are not powerless subject to where the wind blows. Taking that first step in the right direction is the catalyst to stoke the fire that burns for success inside of you. Time goes fast.

One day turns into one month that turns into one year that turns into decades. Create or adopt a sense of urgency and not drag things out. Do not allow negative things like failures in your past to dictate your future. It's time to step on the accelerator and go for it. However, do your research and your homework and soul-search what you want to accomplish. Recruiting a mentor, coach and cheerleader will move things that much faster. The negative chatter will come and attack your mind and get in your face tempting you with fear, doubt and pulling down your spirit.

Don't give in to that chatter. Supplant it with encouraging thoughts, words and take action sooner versus later. I recommend reciting positive affirmations on a daily or regular basis. On your mark, get set now go!

# 17

# Warrior in You

**Dragon of Panophobia (Fear of Everything)**

If you have any hope in living the life you dreamt for all those years, you must adopt a warrior mentality. A warrior mindset that speaks to your soul that quitting is not an option. That spirit that will dig the heals in the ground so deep that the only path you will take is forward, never backward. A never say die attitude.

Warrior?

Am I advocating aggressive behavior? Absolutely not!

Must you have a military background or MMA fighting skills or win the Olympic decathlon? No, you just have to be fundamentality "you" with the commitment to commit to doing all you can do to be where you want to be in this life. You may have to reprogram or reframe your thoughts in order to adopt a new belief system. The basis for this chapter is akin to the expression thick skinned or the phrase toughen up.

My hope is to help you lay the foundation that nothing will stop you. I want you to be impenetrable. No matter how durable the obstacle, no matter how tall that hurdle is you will leap over it in a single bound like the Man of Steel, aka, Superman or Supergirl.

Furthermore, if you cannot leap over that obstacle then you will smash straight thru it not in anger, not in rage but in the highest in confidence and perseverance you can muster. Yes, I know you're not a superhero on film or in the comics but a real, blood flowing within the vein's mere mortal.

In morphing into this new-found warrior, I speak of, your new belief system will include the way you view yourself. You will start using different language much like learning a foreign language. The objective is to be open to accept all the possibilities beyond your current system of belief.

That adage is true. If you keep doing the same thing over and over again not getting anywhere you want to be then don't expect different results. My friends, you must re-program your mind to do something different in order to seize the prize that has eluded you thus far.

Say, "I am a warrior!" "I am a warrior!"

Okay, you shouted, "I am a warrior" and what happened? Except getting energized momentarily absolutely nothing. It will take more than mere words to be that warrior screaming to burst out. But it's a start for sure. Without a warrior spirit you will succumb to the wills of others, carrying their mandates rather than your torch of success.

My focus is to stoke your internal drive or fire to prove your detractors wrong and to reconfirm within yourself that you have what it takes. To digress, if genies were real and you were guaranteed three wishes, what would your wishes be, to be rich, to live in a mansion and to be popular or to make a difference helping people?

I encourage you to be a warrior that will make a difference in this world. No, it is nothing wrong with helping yourself and your family in rising to the top of the mountain, whatever that mountain is, but aim for not only self-gratification but to improve your situation in the context that others may benefit as well.

How do I become a warrior?

Assuming you are ready to move forward in your quest, warriors must have a mission, a target to achieve and a specific goal. In other words what is your thing? If you don't know what that thing is you must do then you must give it careful thought as to what you want to accomplish. In my experience I have seen people crawl, walk and sprint to achieve "a" goal but it was not "the" goal. I encourage you to spend more time on selecting specific goals rather than go wherever the wind blows you. I have done this more than once and it took much longer to hit my target. In some instance my goal was never achieved because of certain factors which I will cover.

If you were a knight in King Arthur's court, in the midst, of the country going to war, the target or goal is to protect, save or expand the kingdom.

What am I saying?

The goal is the focus. All those tactics and strategies centered around the focus are to position you to achieve the goal. Anything other than this single-mindedness warrior approach is a distraction and a deviation of your target and plan of action. Scattered thinking and being unfocused will cause you to mis your target and take you much longer in reaching your goal.

One factor that is pivotal in moving you toward your accomplishment is hopefully, your goal has passion behind it, and is meaningful. Correction, your warrior mentality must have extreme passion or will behind your motivation to realize the target. If you go in with a lukewarm passion; then failure may really mean failure as opposed to learning, then falling then getting backup trying again and again, resulting in minimal to no traction. Without meaningful force, you will take that much longer to achieve the warrior's dream of attaining the goal.

One thing that helped me reflect or conjure up the ultimate warrior persona was to identify with certain warriors in real life, films and books. By using familial warriors, I moved back and forth from fantasy to reality, in other words, my imagination was positively impacted into the limitless possibilities or realm of the kind of warrior I could be in my own life.

My first thoughts of a warrior were that of my late father, Maurice Sylvan Kane Sr. Although he served combat in the Korean War, as an Army Major, that's not why I selected him as my first warrior subject. Again, warrior can be used as a concept, a figurative and not just a literal soldier fighting in distant lands in hand-to-hand combat, albeit my father served in that role quite literally.

My father was strong in spirit and action. He was a resilient man bouncing back from various adversities that life throws at you. Growing up he instilled in me confidence, focus and the ability to chart my own course, although I deviated severely at times.

In reflecting, he could be laughing one moment and the next exerting his authority over me much like a drill sergeant prepping for warfare. Quite honestly, I did not have full appreciation for his teachings all the time but understood the intended benefit he was attempting to absorb in me.

Yes, my father was a tough cookie expecting the best but also demonstrated compassion and significant generosity.

The warrior inside of him taught me discipline. In fairness and to give full credit, I must add my father was in absolute partnership, lock stepped with my mother, Constine Ruth Kane.

Waking up on time like a well-manufactured Swiss Coo Coo clock was the extremely basic of daily rituals bestowed on me and my brother. Waking up meant be ready for school no later than 6am, ready to go. Unlike many of today's parenting, this was non-negotiable, no discussion and with hundred percent cooperation. You may think getting up in the morning on time is trivial, however, being fired for tardiness is a quite common reason adults, with families to feed, and others such as student workers are let go. Not trivial standing in the unemployment line for such an unavoidable little-big thing.

That said, I still practice that be on time habit to work, appointments and events. The early bird may not always capture the worm, but the late bird almost always loses out at the end. Another shade of warrior discipline learned from my father was completing an assignment that I started. That assignment revolved around homework, chores or just a promise made to a friend or family member.

In any case, I learned that once you agree to something you do it. Moreover, if the activity was mandatory all the better that the project must be finished. In any case there was no excuse good enough to withstand the Maurice S. Kane Sr. scrutiny.

Two warriors that I became fond of and used their actions as a basis for my fundamental warrior beliefs included fictional characters such as comic book hero Superman. Traits such as integrity, compassion, heroically saving others and always doing the right thing, overshadowed even his super strength, x-ray vision and indestructibility.

Batman was another favorite that seemed unstoppable despite being human with no superpowers but was blessed with uber agility, technical prowess, and a power of perseverance that never gave into waving the flag of defeat. In terms of nonfictional warriors and saving the best for last, the list is much longer. Martin Luther King, the great civil rights leader was one of the greatest orators in recorded history and a tireless warrior for all people to experience their God given rights to freedoms that were inherited by being human that no one should have to beg or fight.

Other warriors include, Mother Teresa, the missionary and social worker, Madame C.J. Walker, African American entrepreneur, activist and Philanthropist, Mahatma Gandhi, the civil rights leader, Earle G. Graves, founder and publisher of Black Enterprise, Cathy Hughes, founder and Chairwoman of Urban One, Booker T. Washington, educator, activist, author and leader. There are so many more to mention.

In conclusion, strive to be the warrior you were meant to be as you push toward your accomplishments. Take each day by day, learning from the past, focusing on the present and planning for the future.

# 18

# How'd That Work Out

**Dragon of Animotophobia**
**(Regret)**

Have you ever made a spur of the moment impulse decision?

You know those decisions you sooner or later seem to regret. You say, not me to never. Truthfully, we know the answer to that poignant question. Even the elite, you know the type, the brightest of the brightest of us have fallen into the proverbial trap by not thinking things through sufficiently.

Yes, deluding ourselves, rationalizing why we made the decision we made. I should say the foolish, stupid, or insane purchase or bonehead agreement we made but I won't say it. Seeking wise counsel evading our mindscape to potential consequences of our action(s) would have been the right path.

Falling into the dark sea of regret is not good for anyone

especially an eternal optimist let alone those struggling with depression. However, I believe in order to establish a solid foundation of good decision-making skills and thought processes we must do an important thing first. That thing is to push the replay button in your head and analyze the good, bad and the ugly of your regrettable decision.

Essentially, ask yourself, what went right and what went wrong? The key is to be purely honest with yourself. Calm the mental chatter and look through the looking glass objectively as possible.

Be Mr. Spock for this challenging self-deprecating moment in time, in reference to the famed hero in the original Star Trek cinematic universe. To give you a bit of background on Mr. Spock for those unfamiliar. You see Mr. Spock was a Vulcan, a race of physically and mentally superior bipeds.

He is nearly human-like with the exception of pointy ears and basically emotionless behavior, distinguishing him causing him to be defined as humanoid. My long-awaited analogy focuses on his ability to suppress emotions and essentially be the beacon for objectivity which you and I should simulate.

Admittedly it is difficult to divorce oneself from emotion while attempting to embrace neutrality with our actions. The reconciliation between our rational brain and intuition brain or gut may be more theoretical than reality. Deep down I believe we have a feeling if a decision is the right thing to do for us. For example, when we are in the market for an expensive item like a car we get psyched up where the adrenalin is racing nuclear though our veins and do the justification talk in our heads. You know the phrases, "I deserve it", why shouldn't I buy this it is my money. He or she (significant other) bought that expensive thing last week and so forth. However, he is half-human in conflict with his Vulcan self, so internal turmoil plagues him.

Beyond Mr. Spock and the theoretical "what if" scenarios, to bring this home, this chapter is a referendum on making good decisions or making bad choices. We all get to vote on what those two things means to us on an individual basis. However, can there be grey zones depending on the circumstances?

You can make that argument that you made a good decision at the time that turned out to be a horrible decision after the fact. In fact, my take is many people do this to justify their behavior. It gives people an escape exit for screwing up. The problem with this type of thinking is it immediately erases any form of accountability and owning up to the outcome of the decision.

Let's drill it down even further. You want to purchase a car this week. You selected a slightly used (one- or two-year-old) Toyota Corolla LE sedan. You plan on spending no more than $25, 000 making a monthly payment of $300 per month maximum with a $10,000 down payment on the loan. Your preliminary homework tells you this buy would be in your comfort zone. No harm, no foul at this point as it seems reasonable and assuming you budgeted properly.

You hit the car dealer lots with extreme exuberance. You keep to your planned budget like religion, so far so good. Then you somehow happenstance on the car of your dreams. A current model Mercedes-Benz A-Class A for north of $53,000. You initially tell yourself (call it the good voice) "the car is more expensive than you planned, keep walking". Then the other voice tells you, "You deserve it. All the hard work you do, why not? The Jones' aren't better than me. I'm special. Treating myself can't be bad".

You are now in conflict, indecisive and confused. You are relocating to the land of stupefied. Suddenly, a nice salesman approaches you. They are all nice when it comes to separating you from your hard-earned money. It is their job to sale so no harm, no foul. His goal is to redirect you pointing you in "his right" direction. We'll give the nice man a name, Frank gives you all the stats and narrative about your dream car, everything you want to hear.

After 20 minutes, Frank's immediate supervisor walks up and gives you even more information that will guide you to making the only decision expected, to buy the car. As a rosy picture is painted for you that your life will forever change for the best after this purchase. Your willpower begins to disintegrate leaving you close to helpless. You crumble and give in to temptation. You say yes to the dream. Everyone is so happy for you, the salesman, his supervisor on down to the receptionist and janitor. You leave the lot in your new prize smiling and overjoyed showing your new car off to your family and friends. You are the man, in your Wow moment. You paid double than originally planned but who cares? You made it. You arrived, right?

One month later, it's bill paying time. You sit down with the checkbook paying the gas bill – no problem, the electricity bill-no problem, the rent payment-no problem, on and on. You get to the car payment - $550 dollars after putting x amount down, not the original $10k. Your face is grim, smiling is foreign to you. The joy has been plucked … no snatched from your soul but you write the check. Oh, don't forget the increased car insurance bill either. Wait a minute. You verify your checking account balance, and you start to cry as you have one formerly budgeted item remaining … food. Excuse my English but somebody ain't eating today for sure.

Your new budget is short on you shopping at the grocery store to eat for four weeks, leaving you to contemplate what to do for 1 ½ - 2 weeks short of food. Go ask your guardian angel, "where were you in my time of need?" You know what your angel would say? "Freewill baby, free will to chart your own course." Although this story is make-believe this happens to thousands if not millions of people who fail to make a good decision capitalizing on emotions more so on a plan and the facts of limited resources. The above story reeks with regret on various levels.

Other bad decisions that are catastrophic that we won't

get into but serves as a warning, controversial as they may be. These include, marrying the wrong person, overextending your welcome for the wrong person, not completing school, buying an unaffordable home, breaking the law, spending too much money, buying things you don't need, baby-making without adequate financial resources and excessive detrimental decisions over good ones.

In reflection, whether you agree or not, learn how to use wisdom when contemplating the many of life decisions that can either make you or break you. Some mistakes, many of them can be avoided if you use objectivity versus raw emotions thinking things will get better by themselves.

Now you get the chapter title, "How'd That Work Out?

# 19

—

# Mirror, Mirror

**Dragon Of Chronophobia (Fear of Time)**

Mirror, mirror on the wall who is the fairest of them all?

We know that iconic story Snow White the German fairy tale originally published by the Grimm brothers. However, many grew up on the picture book version that added the Seven Dwarfs twist which Walt Disney sanitized and propelled to even greater heights with the 1937 animated musical feature film, Snow White and the Seven Dwarfs.

As the story goes the evil queen hated the reality that someone other than herself could be the greatest and most beautiful. The green eyed monster of jealously embodied her thoughts and actions. The evil queen's spirit was as dark as dark could get spewing hatred as a result of a sentient mirror.

Do not get me wrong in my opinion it was not the mirror's fault. The mirror was essentially responding to a question and answering as a matter of fact, neither good nor bad. The mirror's purpose was to truthfully answer questions posed to it. It is like a friend asking you what day is today. Today is Sunday. A very neutral response. Most people would not make this a capital offense.

What if we had a mirror that could very well talk would you give it credence over your life? Would it determine how you think? What you feel? How you view yourself? What your future will be? The evil queen was a follower and not a leader in this sense. An example is listening to friends or others and allowing them to take you down a road that you wouldn't have taken otherwise if you followed you own heart. No guarantee of that but a strong argument.

As we are fully aware such a mirror does not exist. However, what we tend to do in place of a living sentient mirror is use our minds to reflect a past full of negative memories and emotions. A mind that tells us that we are not good enough or smart enough or the fairest of them all.

When you look in the mirror of your mind what do you see? How do you define yourself? What moniker pops up?

You may either generate warm and fuzzy feelings of joy or haunting reflections of a mistake, an error in judgement, a reflection of falling short perhaps failing to succeed in something or a relational situation calling out to you from the depths of hades itself.

You say, is not there a grey area far removed from either

of the two extremes? Mentally speaking, can't there be a so-so plane of existence neither heaven nor hell but somewhere in the middle like a purgatory? Interesting proposition and tug of war labeling our existence as we look back or foretelling titles as we progress through our lives. Never say never and never say always as the axiom goes.

The way I see it if there is a mere one ounce of poor self-defining going on in your mind then it tilts on the negative reflection versus the positive reflection. Personally speaking, on many occasions, I could not see a third grey or neutral option. Wait a minute what if we compartmentalize and see certain areas of our lives as great then the next area horrible?

For instance, let us visualize we have a great job where we utilize our knowledge, skills and make good money. But our personal life is in shambles framing a lonely and unfilled desire of having that special someone. Okay, I just mentioned my former life of a few years ago.

Also referring to millions of other people playing the on-line dating lottery. There you have it; a segment of your life can be performing to expectations and the other void of joy and happiness. So, what is a person to do amid internal turmoil?

Some form of professional counseling maybe needed to help you move on and push the erase button on that negative framing going on in your mind. However, I am also a proponent of self-development as well.

This quasi-poor/good reflection of the past and semi-optimistic outlook for the future will drag you down. Hence the title of this chapter "Mirror Mirror" denotes the duality we operate from that we carry or rather struggle with each day.

Whatever you focus on you shall certainly bring more of it along for the ride of your life. Suppressing negatives does not work either in my opinion. They will rise again if not dealt with head on. At some point something or someone will trigger that thing you suppressed. Easier said than done, so clichéd but true. How do we move to that place of positive energy? Well, wounds take time to heal. And the deeper the wound the longer the time so says conventional wisdom. Again, professional therapy with a licensed specialist may be required in order to conquer your issues.

When I dealt with my own issues or insecurities, I first had to take time to decipher the negative chatter in my mind that caused my inability to move forward. I self-questioned who do you believe?

Those that put you down or those that support you building you up? Same is true about our two internal beings. Am I listening to my negative me or my positive me? At times, the positive chatter was overrun by the negative. For many years I saw myself as two people -the yes me and the no me. No, I was not delusional. Confusion had filled a void as fear, doubt and gloom occupied my thoughts. At one point in my life all I saw was sunsets. Yet the sun seems to rise again despite those feelings of pessimism. Enough is enough I told myself. I thought okay I have the mirror of the past and the mirror of my future.

Instead of trying to shatter the mirror of my past I embraced it. I used it as a catalyst to motivate my march toward freedom of accepting who I am. Accepting the fact that I am me and to be the best me is all I want to be. This was in the face of one or two people stating, "why don't you be more like so and so? "I eventually developed a powerful vision of what direction I wanted to take my life and better yet my revised self-concept. You cannot just think or will yourself toward success or various levels of achievement without action although I believe it does start with the mind. Those thoughts must manifest into our two-dimensional world.

In other words, the effort to physically reach for your goals must be there at some point. I adopted the concept, "I think who I am" and "you already have what it takes to succeed". I suggest you the reader adopt these types of affirmations or better yet self-fulfilling prophecies as the gospel truth.

Do not get me wrong I am not advocating touchy feelie declarations of falsehood or pretension. Because you say it is so does not mean it will happen. Will gold bullion drop from the sky as manna from the heavens as it once did according to biblical principles? Most likely not but if it did let me know your location cousin. What will happen is the dynamic of cause and effect will initiate. As you start acting on those affirmations or life scripts things will miraculously occur. At the end of the day, you must believe to achieve. So which mirror of thyself will you believe?

By the way, I am moving forward as demonstrated by writing this book which I hope is able to help many others in their walk toward freedom. It will take time although miracles do happen. The point is put in the work, and you will be reaping the rewards.

# 20

—

# Just Once

**Dragon of Phronemophobia (Thinking)**

These two words that make up the title of this chapter have out right destroyed, ruined or setback many of people over the ages. Although, these two words are not necessarily dark or absolute predictions of gloom and doom, they do end up that way more so than not.

In all fairness and being optimistic, there have been many favorable results as well. Case in point, let's say there's man named Sam and he plays a lottery for the first time beginning with the comment, "just once" I'm going to play the lottery. Keeping with this positive spin, Sam declares, "I won, I won $50, 000 dollars. Well, that sounds positive to me. Yes, there can be bold announcements of just once and everyone still has their limbs intact.

Looking at the flip side of Mr. positive, in my observation and experience the two-word phrase typically foreshadows something bad about to happen, at the very least unwelcomed or unpleasant consequence.

What makes this phrase so dangerous and powerful?

Quite simply it gives way to making excuses or an easy open door for not doing what you should or should not be doing. Just once, lends to avoidance of accountability and promotes a conscious disregard for pursuing the direction contrary to the truth or expectant behavior. It's so easy to dismiss these two gentle and soft words as harmless and the attacks against using them as extremist such as Chicken Little, "the sky's falling down" all over again.

Again, to defend myself from potential critics who believe I am just focused on the negative, are there ever harmless situations where expressing them will not cause World War III? Over and above the previous example of Sam winning the lottery, let's take John who is on a diet and is invited to a birthday party where cake is being served. The host offers all the attendees including John a healthy slice of cake.

John initially declines the offer, but the host insists he takes it. John gives in and graciously accepts a slice and eats it. John either accepted it because of a low resistance to temptation or for being a polite grateful guest. Did John commit a great sin? Not hardly, either way John is human and has a right to make his grown-up decisions. One exception that I can think of where it would be detrimental to John is if he had a serious health condition that would preclude certain sugary pastries or deserts where the consequences could be dire, proving my point. So "just once" could lead to an unpleasant outcome with this simple example above.

Let's go back to our childhood where for some people a penchant for trouble or the likelihood of it was patiently waiting right around the corner. Call this example mythical or reality, I will use an example that some can relate to directly. My example involves cookies. If this isn't your history then replace cookies with another choice of disobedience. In your childhood remember mom assertively advising you and/or your siblings, "no cookies until after dinner" or more draconian, "no cookies until the weekend" and its only Monday. Later that night you hear a yell, "who ate the cookies?"

Without warning, your mother lined you all up as you have seen on those detective or crime shows. There are no smiles or expressions of love, just pure good cop, bad cop rolled up in one, about to turn into just bad cop. All those interrogated denied the allegations and silently pleaded the fifth.

In the guilty party's minds, in flashback style you can hear his/her thoughts, "just one cookie and all will be well. Just once I will disobey mother. Is that so wrong?

It's only one cookie and one lie, how bad can that be?" The ultimate punishment was no TV, no playtime, no hanging out with friends, no this and no that and more chores and more parental added homework. Of course, this so-called harmless mental chatter is to sooth your very guilty conscious. To justify the lies and deception writing it off as no big deal. I had friends and acquaintances that played this just once game one too many times and paid a lifelong price as this behavior graduated to greater levels of deceit and painful consequences. You see extreme self-indulgence ultimately leads to poor habits that may not come along with second or third chances to correct the situation or experience.

So how does this just once scenario play out in our personal or professional life as adults?

The answer is nebulous, it depends. The results can be dire to inconsequential. In other words, like a prick on your finger to life-threatening.

To be clear, I don't believe it's a matter of lack of control with the majority of people. In my opinion, it's more a matter of not making good decisions one or too many times, avoiding exercising integrity, and the courage to embrace accountability. I believe many people know the consequences, they are misreading the probabilities for success or failure. They thought about it and betting on lady luck. It wouldn't hurt to possess faith and belief in yourself to take the high road.

However, there are psychopaths who operate on another spectrum and take the just once way too far. They are morbid causing pain and suffering to others while enjoying it. If you think 100% of every human being is essentially good, just watch the crime and investigative shows and you will find certain people without consciouses, souls, and any regard for life. The devil may be taking notes for some of hell bound's finest.

On a personal or relational level this means engaging in honest and healthy relationships. For instance, if you pledge your commitment to a monogamous relationship then don't cheat, refrain from the two-headed beast, you know it's coming … "just once".

It can also be used as an excuse to get out of something, such as to attend a celebration or sporting event. Especially if you are a parent do your best and make every effort to be in your child's life no matter the age. That said, you dodge this very important event for whatever reason by making legitimate sounding excuses. The word I believe is we make white lies. We tell ourselves; I will make this one little lie "just once". Nobody will get hurt.

We're parents till we die. This is not to suggest that legitimate obstacles don't pop up out of the blue. The point is to be upfront with those personal relationships especially if children are involved let alone that bestie who has your back. You should reciprocate the support when able.

Professionally speaking, we must demonstrate consistent high-level commitment to our jobs and careers. That is if we have ambition to rise the so-called corporate ladder. This also pertains to entrepreneurship and business owners as well. In the end, whether tethered to a workplace or conquering the world of maximizing revenue or profits in your business, we all have someone to answer to in order to succeed.

Just once, price gouging a good customer or reducing the widgets included in the typical order is a sign of unethical behavior. Fudging your time sheet just once is another opportunity to stand in the unemployment line making excuses justifying inappropriate and, in some cases, criminal behavior.

In business or in the job the goal is to adhere to proper behavior and to do our best for ourselves, our employers and especially our customers. As an employee, give 110% today and then do 120% tomorrow.

I encourage you to create the habit of using the phrase just once as a positive. We all had those thoughts that irritated us because of our failure to move forward with those thoughts. Act on your dreams and say just once I want to do this or do that and then make plans to do whatever it is you want to do.

You see you can delay a much-needed vacation or opportunity if you don't act on it. I'm not saying to be hasty and irresponsible by just abruptly leaving everything behind. Naturally, plan, plan and plan.

Remember, life is short, so live it just once.

# 21

# Pin Ball

**Dragon of Tropophobia (Making Changes)**

Are you allowing others to dictate your future? Do you feel powerless watching time go by without having a say so in where you want your life to go? Feeling helpless?

Well, you are not alone. Many feel the same way as you do.

I may be dating myself, but I remember in my younger years playing the arcade games in malls with my friends. Back in those days the malls were all enclosed and not open air. I was obsessed with anything arcade. As I reminisce, one game stood out as a fan favorite, the one and only pin ball machine. This game in theory was quite simple.

Here's how it worked. We picked the type of pinball which had themes such as pirates or clowns or spaceships or karate fighters. The most popular games were tough to im-possible to jump on. We put our quarter in the machine. Yes, you heard me a quarter. Try finding anything the price of a quarter and you will die trying. In fact, before we played pin ball we cashed in our dollars for rolls and rolls of quarters, so we didn't have to leave the game. The last thing you wanted to happen was to run out of quarters and have to abandon the game to stand in long lines converting your dollars to quarters. If it was a popular game someone waiting for the chance will step in to play your game.

To activate the game or put it in motion we pulled the springe-controlled handle that would propel a silver metal ball. If we didn't pull the handle back with sufficient strength the ball would embarrassingly return to its starting point.

The goal of the game was for the ball to hit anything in its path multiple times scoring as many points as possible. You wanted the play to continue as long as possible maximizing the duration of play. In theory the game was simple, however in practice difficult. There were obstacles like mazes in the balls path that prevented or blocked us from scoring.

Well to bring the point home, our lives can feel that way. You know ... like pin ball games. As in a pin ball game, you see where the ball needs to go, and you know how the journey starts. It's that path in the middle, from here to there, that is marked with traps and land mines that causes you challenges, defeats and doubts.

In other words, you feel powerless, enslaved and dragging the shackles of bondage wherever you go. Hope is in the distant future in your bleak scenario. So, what should you do? Quite authoritatively, take your power back and sum up the courage to direct your own ship. Listen to you for a change and stop being that metal ball inside the pin ball machine being played by others on what your life should be and how you should get from point a to point b and so forth.

Wow!

That's it, just take my power back. You may be telling yourself? "I'm not strong enough, I'm too weak, no guts at all to make a change." It may take great effort on your part to lead your own way out of the pin ball game, but if you don't stand for yourself, the Calvary ain't coming to save you, pardon my grammar. One thing is for sure, you can't change anyone but yourself. That is a fool's folly just ask someone who made the attempt to change someone else.

Growing up I was wondering what to do with my life. As a young child I volleyed many ideas on the vocation I would choose. Ideas included policeman, fireman, astronaut, musician and so forth. As I got older to teenage-hood, I knew I wanted to do something in business but still unsure, vacillating back and for the between several ideas.

I received input and advice from others which sometimes wasn't advice but them directing me to be something that wasn't in my spirit to be. I was still trying to find me, but I knew I wanted to be successful. It was just the how to get to that point which caused me much consternation. I began to copy, mutate, and turn into someone else other than myself or true being.

Ultimately, I transferred my power or mojo over to other well-meaning souls that wanted me to succeed. The problem with following someone's footsteps or dreams is obvious. It may not be your path. Moreover, even if you are on road to living life large, you are still giving up part of you.

Basically, whose life are you living?

In closing, my ultimate point is seizing ownership, control over your life and direct your life movie. Don't be that metal ball waiting to be thrust into action at the whim of others, bouncing around in the game of life. Assume control over that pin ball game handle and you choose which direction to lead not follow. You have the power.

# 22

# Every Day is Your Birthday

**Dragon of Monophobia (Ignored or unloved)**

I know you are questioning what this title of this chapter has to do with anything relevant to the scope of this book. Well, I am glad you asked. To be captain obvious, in reality; all we have is only one true birthday each year. We typically celebrate this festive occasion with friends and family. Twenty-four hours is all we get to feel extra special and be showered with gifts.

Do you recall a time in your life when everything went right? More so than not that was probably on your birthday. You were ecstatic, smiling all day wishing those feelings and acknowledgements would never end. Outside of Christmas, a graduation or wedding this was not only the day this was your day.

Although you were hoping this day would last forever, toward the sunset of your day the old axiom kicked in that all good things come to an end. Your trip to outer space visiting the Milky Way galaxy was a roundtrip excursion. And then it was over.

I fondly recall when my daughter Matea was five years old, and we visited the Magic Kingdom in Anaheim for her birthday. At that time Disneyland had a program where if it were your birthday, you gained free entry in the most magical place in the world.

Wow!

Free was a great deal. All day from 9am to nearly mid-night employees, park characters and complete strangers were wishing Matea a Happy Birthday.

Did you think Matea felt special?

Again, captain obvious, of course she did. You are most likely saying to yourself how did everyone know it was her birthday? Upon entry the guest or visitor center pins a Happy Birthday button on all the "special birthday guests".

As her father I was very proud of Matea. Each time another park visitor wished her Happy Birthday Matea could not stop smiling and being cheerful. We were all smiling and grateful to participate in her special day.

Regardless, if it is someone's special day or not, we should sow a positive seed into someone's life by treating them as one of a kind. We are all one of a kind, no two alike even for twins, each of us are deserving of feeling like it is our birthday full of joy and support.

This practice can be delivered at home or work or at the store. The setting does not really matter, wherever there are people there is an opportunity to demonstrate compassion, politeness, and encouragement. The Golden Rule comes into play every second of every day we encounter people.

Whatever your vocation in life, teacher, engineer, comedian, professional athlete, minister, postal worker, state employee, mechanic, construction etc. you do not have to be paid as a coach to cheerlead someone on to success as if the day and day is, their birthday.

Will every day be a good day? Most likely not, however, reality with a dose of optimism and seeing the light at the end of the tunnel the cliché goes is a great way to lead. People from all walks of life want or need hope to get through to the next day. We as human beings want essentially the same core things from this life. After the basic necessities from life are met we want to have meaning or purpose as propelled by positive influence. And that positive influence can be you.

However, in order to be that beacon of light for others, you must first have your own bucket filled with that same energy of optimism. Today, or tomorrow could be the best day of your life. In my humble opinion that should be a primary goal. You can self-stimulate your appetite for feeling special by reciting affirmations, meditation and responding to the challenges of life in a positive manner. I am not suggesting practicing self-deception at all. Deal with the blows that life brings but turn those setbacks or failures into success by responding with positive vibrations. You have nothing to lose by viewing the glass as half-full versus half-empty. One last thing,

Happy Birthday!

# 23

# Superhero

**Dragon of Herophobia (Heroes)**

The dragon of herophobia wants us to overlook certain people in our lives.

When it comes to superheroes, we tend to think of the slew of comic book characters or the Marvel or DC Cinematic Universes. In the make-believe world, the fantasy place where anything can happen, or you meet metahumans with remarkable powers.

There are tens of dozens of these heroes from not just over the world but beyond our universe, dimension somewhere in the multiverse. No matter how great these superheroes, they aren't real, only mythical beings we revere.

This chapter is about the heroes that don't always get the credit they deserve. Call them the silent heroes and maybe not appreciated enough by those closes to them. This is not about our typical flesh and blood heroes we always read about or acknowledge, such as sports figures, celebrities, military, fireman, policemen, educators, medical professionals, community leaders, business titans or civil rights activists.

The superheroes I speak of are those everyday heroes that live among us. You are remarkably familiar with the other heroes I refer; you know family, friends, coaches, mentors and others that were with us every step of the way when we had nothing, less than nothing. When others dropped the ball on us, these homegrown heroes were there right by our side. These heroes definitely don't where capes or have utility belts for any incident or catastrophe waiting to happen.

We can be so quick to praise someone we don't even know but forget to thank and speak praises for the people that raised you, fed you, cared for you, financed your existence, and walked with you during those struggles. It may also be true that some people may have only had external popular figures or role models, i.e., celebrities or athletes that enabled them in absentia to succeed or just have hope. I do not want to take anything away from a source of inspiration for others. However, my focus is on the bread-and-butter superheroes that birthed us, trained us, came to our games in school, educated us and supported us directly.

If you asked me who my primary heroes were, I would swiftly tell you without hesitation, my mother and father, Constine and Maurice Kane Sr. Although I did not always tell them that I appreciated what they did for me, I showed them by helping them as they grew older and less able to care for themselves.

I encourage you to show and tell those people who are your personal heroes how much they mean to you. Tell them when you still can and not wait until their funeral. Case in point, do you know when most people receive flowers, plants or gifts of thankfulness? I am not referring to Christmas or their birthday or special occasions.

When they … drum roll please … die. They're delivered at their home, where they no longer reside or at the funeral home where they temporarily reside or at the cemetery where they permanently reside. This is not meant to push a guilt job on you but provide clarity and truth. And undoubtedly giving gifts on special days is a great thing to do.

Again, this is not to diminish anyone or take anything away from the various kinds of heroes out there. My job writing this chapter at this moment in time is to praise and acknowledge the behind-the-scenes heroes. Heroes that may not have invented anything, heroes that sing off-key, heroes that may have not cured any diseases, heroes that have no agility on the court or whatever sports you desire.

My hats off to all the fathers, mothers, siblings, aunts, uncles, mentors, coaches, faith leaders and others too numerous to mention that helped us along so we can be successful or at least have a fighting chance.

# 24

# The Money Game

**Dragon
of Chrometophobia
(Fear of Money)**

Around last Christmas I purchased the board game, "The Game of Life". The game mimics' real life in terms of income, expenses, education, marriage, babies and the type of job you earn wages. As in real life, it throws monkey wrenches at you along the way plus nice surprises. We used to play it when I was growing up. It gave me pause at my young age highlighting how I view life or better yet, what I should do with my life given my goals at that time. Truthfully, I later dismissed some of the prudent teachings of the game, much to my regret.

The game made it abundantly clear that money was at the

center of our very corporeal existence beyond the borders of the game. The simple fact, the more you had in your possession the better off you would be. The accumulation of money meant the building of true wealth which if handled correctly provided opportunities that you could not receive otherwise. Unfortunately, I was not alone in rebuking the wise counsel in this Game of Life. They say misery loves company. Well, I had a lot of company.

This game remarkably throws all kinds of omens and warnings to head for the open receiver and participant of the game. It should be mandatory from middle school to high school. It's one thing to make life mistakes playing a board game rather than blowing up your real life. I wish I could go back and make changes to the path I have taken. Too late for I would've, should've and could've. That reminds me of the classic slow self-destructive debate which you will win and lose at the same time, "what if?"

Don't get me wrong I love my life and I am truly grateful for the learning experiences and the blessings along the way. However, it would have been nice to avoid certain traps of life. Traps such as overspending on homes I couldn't afford, purchasing cars that quickly depreciated, not continuing with academic opportunities, not saving or investing sufficiently upon graduating high school and during those formative years. The largest trap was marrying and trusting the wrong person.

You will go crazy overthinking the past, a past you cannot

change no matter how many what if and would've, should've, could've scenarios you dare to playout in your mind. Yes, it's time to move on. I recommend re-reading my chapter Mirror, Mirror. In terms of money, what has the previously mentioned have to do with my current state of financial well-being or your view of money in your life?

The point is you can only start from where you are now. It comes down to making good decisions moving forward. Despite the mistakes of the past the sun shall rise tomorrow, giving way to future endless possibilities. In essence today is the best place to start building your financial independence. Although, I am not finished with my own accumulation of money and journey, I am closer than ever in realizing more of my goals.

Will winning in a board game such as the Game of Life result in prosperity or guarantee success? Or losing that same game spell eternal financial ruin?

Not hardly, like Rocky Balboa, in the highly successful boxing franchise, where the famed boxer was periodically knocked down. Starring Sylvester Stallone, the Italian Stallion as he was affectionately called, popped right back up despite the fierce opponents pummeling him. He was no mere mortal, demonstrating what you can do if you go the distance and persevere. If life throws you a hard uppercut (unexpected expenses) and then a jab to the ribs (life altering event), the same holds true for you by getting right back up continuing to fight for what you want and believe as well. By moving forward and pushing through you can restart your journey to financial freedom. This chapter was not meant to be a full course on personal finance or investments, but I will cover the basics.

## Budget

In order to get your financial house together, it is vitally important to know where your money is going. This is easily accomplished by tracking your monetary inflows and out-flows. Once you gather this information, then it's the matter of assigning the numbers that represent living within your means. If you earn $20 dollars, the goal is not to spend $20 or leverage over that and spend $25.

Prior to this point, your money has been sucked through a black hole. Knowing that fact, you must change your behavior to accommodate the future prosperous you where your financial freedom lies. There are various apps out there that will help you track your income and expenses. Every Dollar by Dave Ramsey and Mint are the first that comes to mind.

## Emergency Fund

In your money journey you need to establish six months to one year savings for an emergency fund. The emergency fund will provide for your essential needs. This account is for any surprises that come your way such as job loss, car repair or home maintenance, hospital bill etc. It is vitally important your family's needs are met, i.e., water, food, clothes, shelter and so forth.

Actually, these essential needs are outlined in Abraham Maslow hierarchy of needs paper. Maslow was a psychologist by trade. His hierarchy of needs was published in his 1943 paper" A theory of Human Motivation" in the journal Psychological Review.

You may have learned this in school. At the bottom it states the most basic needs are physiological needs. This includes air, water, food, shelter, sleep and clothing. The next level is Safety needs which includes personal security, employment, resources, and health. Now the top three levels do not directly come with a price tag or allow saving money, but they might impact your ability to earn money and provide for yourself and family. Love and belonging are on the next level. It involves friendship, intimacy, family, and sense of connection. The second to the top level is esteem. This it tied to respect, self-esteem, status, recognition, and strength.

Hopefully, you have or will attain the highest level of self-actualization. This final step is powerful and speaks volumes to your dreams becoming true as it relates to your desire to become the most that one can be. Most of everything I mentioned above comes from Abraham Maslow not me. Although for the doubters, there may be no scientific basis for his theory, one could hardly argue that these elements are important and necessary for your survival and potential opportunity to prosper. I take it seriously and encourage you to do the same so that you may experience all that life has to offer.

Needless to say, this fund should be untouchable unless an urgent need arises stated in the examples above. The goal is also not to tap into your retirement account or college fund for your children.

## Debt

Whatever your situation, you must rid your life of that nasty four-letter word called debt. I know you hear from some experts that some debt is good debt and others bad. Good debt has been called home purchasing or college tuition, akin to an investment versus liability. Although without a doubt buying a home or college attendance are good causes given your choices are within your income limits and doesn't violate living within your means. However, debt is debt is debt. Bad debt is typically credit card debt involving spending sprees for purchases of products and services that you want and do not need. Bad debt is buying an immediate depreciating car that you cannot afford but you bought it because you deserve it – really?

Bad debt is most anything you did not save for in cash, and it is not an essential part of living. Being heavy in debt or having money problems and not being on the same page with your significant other is the number one cause of divorce and domestic issues. The popular song by Tina Turner, what's love got to do with it will replace your most listened tune. Money issues destroy marriages, friendships, peace, the quality of life and possibly the length of life as well. Unbearable stress on the mind, body and spirit can take its toll. Unfortunately, I speak from much experience in this area. Take the red pill of knowledge and rebuke the blue pill of ignorance. I used the Matrix before in this book because nothing beats that analogy.

If you don't head this warning, you will lose years of your life in nightmares and possibly divorce and/or bankruptcy court. Also, your dreams of living a prosperous life will be dramatically delayed or destroyed. Eliminating debt from your life should be your top interest as soon as possible. Don't fall in this trap of extending this or any debt.

### Savings Fund

To have a stable life you must adopt or create the habit of saving a percentage of your income on a regular basis. As debt adds up so will your savings accounts if met with the same or superior level of enthusiasm. There is no one size fits all magic number. I recommend saving as much as possible. That can mean, 5%, 10% or more. Just be honest with yourself and save, save and save not giving in to any excuses.

Of course, this sounds simpler than it is, but it is not impossible to do. If you have to start with $5 dollars, then do it. Get in the habit and then watch your money grow. As your income increases then save even more, not spending those raises or bonuses or side hustle money. I suggest you name your savings goals even in separate accounts if possible. For instance, I have a vacation fund, a car repair fund, a gift fund and so forth.

## Investments

Now that you secured your basic economic foundation, it is time to invest some of that hard-earned money. As previously explicitly stated, your basic needs must be met first. I cannot overstate this fact as some people have violated the hierarchy of needs and put all their eggs in one basket or the wrong baskets and the basket blew up where all was lost. Don't be foolish or overoptimistic with your day to day living your life money.

My purpose is to inform you of the different types of investments. It's up to you to take it one step further and investigate what is right for you. I am merely opening the door to future opportunities. I am not giving financial advice just my opinion and sharing my experience.

I encourage you to have a wealthy mindset and eliminate poor and poverty thinking and embrace a better way for you and your family to not only survive but to thrive. Notice I said eliminate poor thinking and I never mentioned the word broke. My point is poor and broke are not the same thing.

You see broke is a temporary state of existence while poor is a losing state of mind. When you're broke is just means you have no money at this time. Broke equals light at the end of the tunnel because you have a plan to change your situation.

Alternatively, when you're poor you are in a prolonged situation where there is no way out of being poor with no money. Many people in the poor category usually lost hope or may have been put in this situation involving forces out of their control and succumbed to the notion that they are helpless. In the end the mind is very powerful. It directs you as you think and believe.

## Stocks

A great investment is in individual public stocks. If you are new to investing let me, explain. Stock is ownership of a company. You trade your money for a piece of the company pie. Now, as an owner of McDonalds does that mean you can walk into a McDonalds and start telling the managers and staff what to do? No, owning its stock does not give you hamburger flipping privileges.

By owning stocks, you hope that the price appreciates over time making your shares in the company more valuable than the day your purchased them. For many investors, the ultimate goal is to buy low and sell high. For other investors like me the goal is to buy and hold progressively building wealth by holding on for the long term. The public stock of a company is bought and sold on a stock exchange. There are various exchanges in not only the United States but the world. Let's take the New York Stock Exchange (NYSE) as an example. The NYSE is a platform where companies can sell their stock to the general public which is you and me.

Buying stocks come with a price which fluctuates for a variety of reasons. These reasons can be pure supply and demand based on good or bad news such as a new product or invention, or confidence in the leadership of the company, or a scandal breaks loose causing the stock price to spiral. The price can even go up or down for reasons that have nothing to do with the company. The fact is the price may fluctuate for all kinds of reasons.

Buying stocks is how many of the millionaires and billionaires of the world became wealthy. It is time to take calculated and researched risks by investing a percentage of your hard-earned money for growth. Please notice the term risk. If you want to grow your money you cannot get around experiencing some percentage of risk. There is no investment that does not have some measure of losing your money or a level of devaluation.

You must get educated about what you are investing. There are thousands of books on the subject of stock investing and other possible categories of investments. There are hundreds of YouTube channels dedicated to the subject as well. However, your focus should be to put learning as the top priority.

The 401k or pre-tax equivalent vehicle at your job is one of the best places to start because the invested money is pre-tax. This means your taxes owed will be reduced and you will probably earn more money because you have more money working for you. Check with your human resource department on signing up.

Outside of a job-based investment program, I recommend choosing a low-cost provider such as Fidelity, Vanguard, or Acorn. There are many to choose from so do your homework. Investing in index or exchange traded funds or even plain vanilla mutual funds would be a good place to initiate your wealth building program as they will save you a lot of money from paying excessive fees.

I would be remiss in not covering the concept of time. The earlier you start investing, then the more time you have for your money to grow. There is a phenomenon called compounding interest. Overtime your money will exponentially grow beyond your initial investment. There can be a huge difference in returns between a twenty-something investor and someone in their forties given all things equal. You cannot buy time or grow time. Now, that doesn't mean all hope is lost for us middle-aged to senior investors. We may have to put larger amounts in to catch up but never say it's too late. You can only start where you start. The point is to act sooner versus than later. The dragon of procrastination is alive and well. Do your best to eliminate this creature from your life as soon as possible as it is robbing you and your family of time, energy and money.

## Bonds

A more conservative and less risky type of investment

vehicle is bonds. The bond is an instrument of indebtedness. A bond is when a company or government entity borrows money from you and me who are called the lender or investor. The two most common types include municipal bonds and corporate bonds. Like many loans, bonds are a contract that have maturity dates. That means the borrower must repay the money to the investor.

Why would you lend money to a bond issuer? Great question. From the point you lend the money to the time your capital is returned; you will receive interest. In other words, you hope to receive a reliable stream of income. In most cases investors with modest investment amounts buy bonds via the more affordable mutual funds. If you are beyond modest means, you may invest directly with the entity or through a broker dealer serving as a liaison.

The biggest problem with bonds is inflation and opportunity cost of investing in an asset class that will beat inflation. At present, bonds are dying on the vine. Case in point, let's say your bond is paying 5%. Consider you have to pay taxes and inflation eroding your interest earned. There is much debate on the real rate of inflation. First, let's define inflation. According to Wikipedia, "In economics, inflation refers to a general progressive increase in prices of goods and services in an economy. When the general price level rises, each unit of currency buys fewer goods and services; consequently, inflation corresponds to a reduction in the purchasing power of money."

There is the official rate of 6.2% through October 2021 that many argue leaves much out of what should be considered or measured. That argument is beyond the scope of this book. Some critics peg the actual rate of inflation at 14%. Wow! In any many people are losing money in bonds because they are not keeping up with the real cost of goods. Something to keep in mind.

## Mutual Fund, Index and Exchange Traded Funds

I am going to touch briefly on investing in these three vehicles, regular mutual funds, index, and exchange traded funds. For those investors that don't have the time, stomach, or talent for investing in individual stocks these three alternatives may be what the wealth doctor ordered.

## Mutual Funds

A mutual fund pools money from many investors to buy stocks, bonds, or other securities. They are professionally managed and sell to retail investors like you or me and institutional investors such as large corporations, endowments, or family offices. The traditional mutual fund is usually the most expensive charging fees for their services. There are a large variety of funds that focus on general investments and others that are tightly focused on a certain sector, i.e., utilities or technology companies.

## Index Funds

Now, an index fund is a mutual fund created to track a

specific basket of underlying investments. There are many types of index funds to choose. For example, a fund can track the S&P 500 which is made up of the largest companies. Basically, you are investing in the market itself. Others can track the Dow Jones Industrial Average, a smaller benchmark of thirty companies or reach abroad to international investing and so forth. Index funds can focus on any type of investment. Popular companies to purchase index funds are Fidelity and Vanguard. Exchange Traded Funds or ETF for short, are essentially index funds with a positive twist. ETFs can be traded throughout the day equivalent to stocks. In contrast to index funds which can only be bought and sold at the end of the trading day. Therefore, there is a delay for index funds.

### Real Estate

The subject of real estate is beyond the scope of this book. This is only a primer to help kick start your investing into the various opportunities that await you. Like with stocks there are various methods or strategies to invest. The most basic that comes to mind is single family homes. To clear something up. The house you live in is not an investment it is a liability and a safe haven for a place to live.

Now this very same house can turn into an investment if you move out and rent it to someone. It would be prudent to not mix or confuse the two interpretations of your home. Also, be cautious not to leverage where you live with debt. If something goes wrong, you can lose your home and become homeless not a good place to be. So don't get tied up in get rich quick schemes that are designed by definition to depart your hard-earned money from your pockets. What makes me so smart or experienced in this matter. Well, been there and done that. I was in foreclosure before being overleveraged, i.e., too much debt than I could financially afford or handle. So, let's move on.

### Single Family Homes (SFH)

SFHs can be an excellent choice as long as you don't overbuy where the numbers don't make sense. The money is in the buy and not the sell. I'm not going to cover flipping houses, but investors can make a decent living on buying, fixing up and reselling direct to the homeowners or whole-sale investors.

But let's say you want to be a long-term landlord and have no interest in buying. That's fine, however, plan your budget and determine what is viable so you make money every month in order to pay the bills. There will always be expenses that come with real estate investing. A danger here if you don't sufficient resources. For example, in an SFH you only have one tenant and if something happens to that one tenant and you have a mortgage then you will have to tap into your reserves. If you but it free and clear, then you have much more flexibility.

I know an investor who has several homes. This is great because she has sensible mortgages on all her properties, and she did her due diligence and have good tenants with a work ethic and sense of morality that helps her take care of the properties. That leads to a point. It is vital that you screen your prospective tenants with all your strength and might.

This is personal and business, you must ensure you have renters that will view your relationship as a partnership. In turn, the rent is rarely raised beyond a certain percentage, and she adds upgrades where feasible resulting in pride of ownership without them being owners. Other forms of investing can be in manufactured housing or mobile homes, townhomes, or condos. I will add duplexes, triplexes and four-plexes, in the realm of residential type investments. The main point with the plexes is that you can live in one of the units while renters will pay for the whole property resulting in you paying minimal to zero payments out of your pocket for a place to live. These are viable alternative to stand alone SFHs.

### Multi family

These typically are apartments ranging from five and more units. These properties are called commercial property versus SFH residential. There are various types of styles to types which I won't cover. The bottom-line is this form of investing can accelerate your wealth if you buy right and have the right kind of tenants. Also, you may need partners with apartment investments as they don't come cheap. They may require some degrees of rehab and definitely ongoing maintenance as with every real estate investment. However, this is multiplied by the number of units.

## Non-Direct Ownership

This entails not actually owning the direct properties. There is a way to not get your hands dirty by investing in tax liens. In this type of investing, you are buying the paper on taxes owed to a government entity. Many states provide auctions or over the counter selling of tax liens. When you purchase the lien, you can get 5% to over 30%. And after a certain period if the delinquent homeowner does not pay it off you may be able to actually receive the property after due diligence.

## Tax Deed

This is contrast with tax deed investing. In this type of investing if you enter an auction against other bidders, you may end up with a property at the auction if you are the winning bidder. This is still under direct ownership.

## Real Estate Investment Trusts

The last topic on the subject of real estate investing. There is a way to participate in real estate investing bypassing the potential headaches of buying and renting property. Real Estate Investment Trusts or REITS for short are an excellent method of being in the real estate game. I personally own several with my wife and through our company. Wit REIT investing these companies pay regular dividends along with possible price appreciation. Many companies like McDonalds will pay you five dollars per share or more and some less.

There are three types of REITS:

1. Equity – direct ownership, operating property, and renting.
2. Mortgage – lend money to real estate investors.
3. Hybrid – investing, managing property and lending.

REITS invests in all types of real estate. Most specialize in certain sectors of the economy. Here is a list of investment types:

- Apartments
- Single Family Homes
- Shopping Centers
- Hotels
- Motels
- Manufacturing
- Warehouses
- Office buildings
- Data Centers
- Cell Towers
- Agriculture

**Cryptocurrency (crypto)**

What is crypto?

Succinctly, a digital asset designed as a medium of exchange. More comprehensively, per Wikipedia,

"a cryptocurrency, crypto-currency, or crypto is a collection of binary data which is designed to work as a medium of exchange. Individual coin ownership records are stored in a ledger, which is a computerized database using strong cryptography to secure transaction records, to control the creation of additional coins, and to verify the transfer of coin ownership. Cryptocurrencies are generally fiat currencies, as they are not backed by or convertible into a commodity. Some crypto schemes use validators to maintain the cryptocurrency. In a proof-of-stake model, owners put up their tokens as collateral. In return, they get authority over the token in proportion to the amount they stake. Generally, these token stakers get additional ownership in the token over time via network fees, newly minted tokens or other such reward mechanisms."

Crypto's utilize a blockchain in order to operate. **What is a Blockchain? In summary, a digital database.**

**Per Wikipedia, it's longform definition is the following:**

"A blockchain is a growing list of records, called blocks, that are linked together using cryptography. Each block contains a cryptographic hash of the previous block, a timestamp, and transaction data. The timestamp proves that the transaction data existed when the block was published in order to get into its hash. As blocks each contain information about the block previous to it, they form a chain, with each additional block reinforcing the ones before it. Therefore, blockchains are resistant to modification of their data because once recorded, the data in any given block cannot be altered retroactively without altering all subsequent blocks."

Those who are creating their versions or vision of currency utopia hope to enable a system free of any governmental or private control. Some are anarchist others just wanting to be independent of fiat rule. Not to get too deep into the topic of economics, the U.S. dollar and other world currencies are steadily losing their value as many world governments continue to print money without abandonment and no regard of future valuations and diminished purchasing power. Moreover, many world currencies are pegged to the dollar. So, wherever we go they go, good or bad. Crypto may be the answer to freedom from the debasement of the various currencies.

### Asset Class

Regardless, if accepted as a currency alternative, crypto is presently tagged an asset class such as a stock. That said, like a stock if you buy one share at $10 and sell it at $20 then that will trigger a capital gains tax assessed on the $10 difference. Just replace share with token or coin. There are many types of crypto that hope to be of utilitarian value to make things better and faster and most accurate, transparent as can be.

Currently Bitcoin is the elephant in the room. Others

include, Ethereum, ADA, Chainlink, XRP, and XLM to name a few. Tokens are identified in categories such as gaming. An example is Mana which is linked to the crypto Decentraland, Sands is tied to Sandbox, the token Matic which is attached to Polygon and Gala (crypto and token) where their native token is paid or earned in their specific ecosystem. There are thousands of crypto and tokens. You must do your homework for sure.

### Crypto Exchanges

To purchase cryptocurrencies, you must join a crypto exchange. This is like buying a McDonalds's stock via a broker on the New York Stock Exchange. There are many exchanges to choose depending on your intentions. Not to endorse any specific exchange, I personally use Coinbase and Binance USA. I like each companies' platforms, fees, payment methods, reputation, and customer service.

Non-Fungible Tokens have caught on fire over the last few months. To remain hip and cool, they are called NFTs for short.

### What are NFTs?

They are digital content that are connected to a blockchain. The digital content could represent ownership in collectibles, music, artwork, videos, images, or virtual real estate. NFTs are unique and cannot be exchanged like money trading hands. NFTs are currently blowing up especially in the artwork and virtual real estate. Investors are spending thousands to millions on virtual real estate. I am neither here to persuade or dissuade if this is prudent or otherwise. I recommend you do serious research and invests as you are able to do without jeopardizing your financial future. This realm of investing is highly speculative so only spend what you can afford to lose which is the case with all investments.

## Metaverse

One thing for sure that has been capturing the attention of the crypto community, investors, the public and the general media has been our future new way of life which is the metaverse. This will be where we live, sleep, work and have fun if you believe the news or the hype. It will be a place we gather to commune with our co-workers, friends, and family. The business community at large is hoping the metaverse will be a place to advertise, market, promote as people shop for products and services and to transact various business activities. The music industry has already tested the waters for concerts.

Per Wikipedia, "the **metaverse** is a hypothesized iteration of the Internet, supporting persistent online 3-D virtual environments through conventional personal computing, as well as virtual and augmented reality headsets. Metaverses, in some limited form, have already been implemented in video games such as *Second Life*. Some iterations of the metaverse involve integration between virtual and physical spaces and virtual economies. Current metaverse development is centered on addressing the technological limitations with virtual and augmented reality devices. The term "metaverse" has its origins in the 1992 science fiction novel *Snow Crash* as a portmanteau of "meta" and "universe." It has since gained notoriety as a buzzword for promotion, and as a way to generate hype for public relations purposes by making vague claims for future projects. Information privacy and user addiction are concerns within the metaverse, stemming from challenges facing the social media and video game industries as a whole."

An excellent example of the metaverse is seen in the 2018 film, "Ready Player One". It was directed by Steven Spielberg which lends instant credibility from a theatrical point of view. I believe the films has merits from a prophetic standing as to a glimpse to our possible future, at least portions of it. Basically, the film was about a man creating his virtual reality called the Oasis. This creator established a posthumous contest for contestants or shall I say combatants competing to find his Easter egg. The victor will win the man's fortune and control of his virtual reality world, making the winner nearly omnipotent and very powerful.

The contest brings out the good guys as well as the devils. In some cases, it was a thin line between who's good or bad as when absolute power is at stake people can turn into something they ordinarily would not become. A sub-lesson as to human nature if there's an opportunity to essentially rule the world. I do recommend watching the movie to help define what our metaverse should look like and things we probably should avoid.

In terms of investing in the metaverse, there are companies that are building or plan to build their metaverses. You can invest in the gaming companies directly through the crypto exchanges. There are many companies in this space. They include Sandbox, Decentraland, Gala, Axie Infinity, Enjin and others. There are public companies that are providing their expertise or contributing to the building of this third iteration of the Internet. Big companies such as Microsoft, Meta Platforms, Inc. (formerly Facebook), Nvidia, Unity Software, Inc., Autodesk and over hundred other companies. You can buy them individually or via the Roundhill Ball Metaverse Exchange Traded Fund.

I invested in this exchange in the fall of 2021as I viewed it more efficient buying through a fund versus an individual basis which is much costlier as well. Again, this is my opinion and sharing information and to financial advice as you need to conduct your own research and make your own prudent decisions. In any case, check it out and determine if you want to participate as an investor or creator in the future makeup of how we live, both play and work. Sci- Fi for sure.

## Old School

Let's take a brief blast to the past for a moment to reflect, please indulge me.

In the early days of the technological revolution of the twentieth century, analogue was the king. Tape, ribbon, vinyl records, stereo players, VHS and paper were its ambassadors. Cables, transistors, and rabbit ears were the close cousins. A bit before my time the radio was the giant which was supplanted by the black and white television and then color took over. Pre-Internet you had to walk, drive and snail mail everything over to your intended recipient. Back then we can still buy products cash on delivery. That was when payment was delayed until they knocked on your door to deliver your order.

Walkie Talkies were popular. So were board games and other assorted games that promoted in person activities designed to bring family, friends and even strangers together. Then there came pagers or beepers as they were called that allowed us to stop what we were doing and find a telephone booth; you know the thing that Superman changed his clothes from Clark Kent to his superhero outfit.

Back in the day we had to keep a lot of quarters and dimes in our pockets if we wanted to call someone away from the home. There were no cellphones, but the beepers at least notified us that someone wanted to speak with us. Then innovation starting to unfold and accelerate displacing things we once knew as sacred. The early cellphone arrived on the scene, big and bulky at first followed by the flip phone small to place in your pocket.

VHS tapes come to mind watching your favorite movie

that you recorded on these players. Before then your only choice was to physically go to the theater which was a great thing to do.

But that third choice popped up called Blockbuster Video. A destination that enabled you to rent or buy your favorite movie or to take a gamble on a movie you wouldn't pay to go see in the theater. I almost applied to be a franchisee of Blockbuster. I did become an investor. You know how that turned out. Anyone say Netflix?

The telephone booths started to disappear not before the private pay phones were ripping us off before the cellphones gained in popularity. Computers had already existed but not for the common person or home. Then personal computers hit the scene along with word processors which replaced the typewriter. As time move on all sorts of gadgets came like the Sony Walkman, CDs, DVDs and among other fancy things we couldn't live without. Bookstores were proliferating, remember those places that had lot of books? Super Crown, Waldens, Borders and the last of the majors Barnes N' Noble has a lifeline remaining. Too stubborn to die which I am more than overjoyed.

Oh, do I miss walking into a music store, wow! What an experience. Sam Goody, Virgin, Tower Records, Warners, and many others. These places were destination events where friends gathered and they were an expected place to take a date, browsing through books or records. We spent hours and hours.

Then the Internet caught on and finally a full blast of

digitization in the form of software, digital video, gaming, digital images, social media, a proliferation of websites and online retail made analogue but a memory. For an in-depth analysis or commentary on the subject I recommend buying books or viewing YouTube as there is no shortage of pundits or advocates discussing it.

Actually, I just started heavily investing in crypto early this year. I waited on the side lines for this fairly new type of investing. I believe it's been around for about ten years more or less.

There has been much debate on if it is a scam or a legitimate investment. Truthfully, when I first heard about crypto years ago, I didn't know what to think or who to believe. I know one thing I was scared of losing my money.

I am not advocating or dissuading you from investing in crypto. Just do your homework and make up your own mind. I believe it is here to stay and may turn out to be a viable option of growing wealth. That said, investing in a book or two about investments is very prudent. There are numerous books on investing in stocks and real estate and other investments. Read books from Dave Ramsey, David Bach or Suzie Orman are great reads and will definitely put you in the right directions. They face criticisms for their styles and philosophies, but they saved me from more pain and misery. I am on my way for sure.

I also recommend a good read, "Crypto Revolution" by Bryce Paul, and Aaron Malone. This book provided good insight and helped me have the confidence to jump into the world of crypto. Another excellent book is "Bitcoin and Cryptocurrency" by Nicholas Scott. This book accelerated my knowledge and expanded my involvement in this space. It is a 3 - books in 1 resource, tripling your investment in your crypto knowledge for the price of purchasing one book.

In closing, don't wait for your fear to go away before starting your financial freedom journey. Press through the fear and keep moving forward. Take care.

Happy investing!

# 25

# Conquering The Giants

**Dragons of Megalophobia (Large Objects)**

Life is full of challenges and roadblocks. If you aim to achieve any modicum of success, you must clear the field of the giants in your life both personally and professionally. Giants are those things or people that get in our way of realizing success as we define success. In fact, the giants intersect every area of your life.

No, not the New York Giants, the highly respected football team and not the Goliath in the Bible. Although there are similarities as to the giants' I refer which are powerful and intimidating. Obstacles are unfortunately part of our lives. In my workshops or other speaking engagements, I typically ask my audience this question, "does anyone have a carefree life, with no problems or obstacles blocking your path?" So far, no one to date as yelled out or softly whispered a negative response. Even if they had it would not be the truth.

Let's face it no one is perfect although some claim to be via their declarations and pronouncements of godhood. We all got "it", that something that is not right in our lives. As members of the human race, the giant's will come your way. If you live long enough you will experience problems or un-invited lessons to learn.

The giants seem to find us like magnets finding something to cling on. Alternatively, we sometimes create our own problems because we are imperfect creatures. The bottom line is you cannot hide from them. You see giants do not sleep and they do not tire of trying to stop you, feeding on pain and suffering.

Remember the Rocky Balboa movies?

Film after film had Rocky getting pummeled, taking hit after hit, and bloodied up prior to him ultimately being victorious. You may be thinking I am alluding to you getting in a boxing ring. Yes, you are correct. Figuratively of course and not literally. To get to that next level you must get in the boxing ring of life facing your Goliath.

First you must identify and recognize your giants. Sometimes you may be unaware of them until you take those steps to move forward with your life. You see on some occasions only until you enter the boxing ring do you realize the true giant blocking your path wasting your precious resources and time.

In many instances, the giants may seem like the goals themselves but that is not usually the case. For example, let us imagine for a moment you have a goal of losing 30 pounds by next summer. After some self-inflicted emotional turmoil, you convince yourself that your goal is impossible. Your focus is 30 pounds. However, in reality, the giant is actually something underneath, hidden, or sinister. The real enemy here could be a number of things.

First comes to mind is the source behind the negativity or the doubt that you can realize your 30-pound weight loss. Perhaps you feel discouraged because your past is checkered with giving up before your goal was achieved. Another goal buster is feeding into the lies that someone gave you that you are not good enough.

You could also be comparing yourself with others whereas you firmly formed a competitive spirit in your mind with someone you feel is your superior or you are less than their equal. The point is that we face a choice. Every day we make decisions that either elevate or diminish. We go left when going right was the better of the two. This is the case in many instances when we knew in our hearts and mind the direction to take. This may be attributable to fear.

Why would someone do that intentional misdirection? Because he or she is familiar and comfortable and is more scared of the unknown than the known. Some call it the devil I know versus the one I don't know.

If the giant is greater than our want or our need then we will not realize our goal and our purpose. Let's take our 30-pound weight loss goal further. Initially, we are gung-ho, extremely excited at the prospect of losing weight and becoming the person we always wanted to be.

Then for some reason that desire to lose weight starts to fade into a faint memory after high levels of energy and much time was spent. Perhaps achievement of our goal is taking much longer than we anticipated. For example, what if you only lost three pounds after busting your butt? No one would disagree that losing a low nominal weight can be disappointing.

Or perhaps we backslid and cheated overloading on those spicy chili fries from your favorite fast-food place. Instead of losing 10 pounds you gained 15. Setbacks are quite natural. Discouragement can be expected to some degree. The difference between success and underachievement is perseverance and not giving up before the race is over.

How do I know if I'm winning or losing the game of life?

Good question.

Back to perseverance. You may appear to be losing your race for whatever goal is you seek. Maybe things do seem dire and as hopeless as hopeless can be. Maybe you got your butt whipped 9 out of 10 times with 5 minutes left on the clock. The answer to the question lies within you.

If you tell yourself the game is over then it is over. If you tell yourself that the game is only beginning, then you give opportunity a chance to replace losing the victory cup in your life. You have more power than you think.

Clichéd or not, do not give up. When you give up it is not just giving up on an idea, or a wish, you are giving up on you. You need to revitalize that burning desire or passion you once had to get you to the top of the mountain.

Don't believe the lie that you are not smart enough, good enough or worthy. Remember all it took was a slingshot and a rock for David to defeat Goliath, the giant in his life. But was it just a slingshot and a rock? Not really. David had hope, faith and belief which was represented by those instruments he used to overpower his giant.

That said, you can do the same. Each day you wake up for the day, you have achieved your first victory for the day. Whisper to yourself that it can only get better from where you start. The most important thing is it is where your finish and not start.

# 26

# A Feather is Still

**Dragon of Decidophobia (Making Decisions)**

I know this chapter title is strange. Stay with me for a little while and I will fully explain., hopefully taking a short road approach.

Here goes ...

A feather is still a feather whether on purpose or by accident. Okay, getting even stranger. Peculiar to say the least.

If you release a feather when a gust of air is present, what happens? Come on, give me your best guess.

The current of air will carry that feather in the direction of the wind. If the wind goes east, the feather goes east. If the wind travels northbound then the feather tags along in that direction and so forth. You see the feather is not in control of its situation almost at any time of its existence. The feather is beholden to the winds. It is left to the mercy of the wind.

The feather is a servant to the master wind. The wind dictates everything the feather does or accomplishes every moment the feather exist. Each day the feather is activated by motion initiated by the wind. It still must comply with its master never charting its own independent course. Minute by minute, hour by hour, day by day and so forth, the feather must answer to the wind.

You may be asking what the heck does this diatribe have to do with me? Others may already see themselves as either the feather or the wind depending on your individual circumstances and life story. However, it is my guess that the majority of readers feel one way or another.

To further break it down, regarding your life do you ever feel like the feather so described above? Do you ever feel that you have no control or say so in your present or future? Do you feel like a slave bound by your circumstances, never free from the shackles of obedience to a master?

My friends if you ever had these feelings, you are not alone. I have felt this way for many, many years. I felt trapped, despondent, with no sense of inner purpose or joy. A boat without a rudder was my life. Millions of people have travelled down this dark road, and many are just starting out this road to nowhere.

How did we get on this road?

First let's go over who we need to be to play the cards we are dealt in a productive manner. We were born with a purpose for our lives. Our birth, this was no mistake. As the months rolled by, we learned many things like crawling and then stumbling as we made our first attempt to walking. In those early months we were glued to our bottle. It was our trusted companion. Wherever we went that warm bottle followed. Then one of our first experiences of loss was that bottle being stripped from our very grasp as we weaned off of it to bigger and brighter beverage cups and receptacles. One chapter of our lives abruptly ended while a new chapter opened up.

Yes, we gave a mighty and powerful fit when our baby bottle was taken by force. We were overwhelmed by negative emotions. Absolutely miserable feelings for sure. But what happened next? We began to forget that loss and embraced our new lives with various cups and containers not thinking twice about losing our baby bottle. We eventually adapted and moved on to newer and bigger mountains to climb like learning to climb out of our crib or crawl upstairs. I'll cover that in the next book.

What is my point?

We need to be that baby we once were long, long time ago.

This is not a time to place blame but an opportunity to get off this path and find the road you should be travelling on to meet your true calling. This chapter is not about feathers and baby bottles, it is about taking control of your life and using your rudder to steer you in the right direction. We need to decide which direction to take our lives. It's okay not to have all the answers at once. However, there should be some energy of thought to get started.

How do we get our control back is the million-dollar question?

I promise you if you don't control your life someone else will most definitely. You see if you acquiesce or cede leadership over to someone else, they will determine your lot in life. Now, occasionally that may benefit you if you have a good or great person supporting you and being your posse. When I said supporting, I don't mean financial. I mean emotionally, psychologically, and spiritually.

Sometimes, perhaps many times, the person taking control could be in our very own nuclear family. Your father, mother, siblings, or grandmother living with you. They may mean well and really want you to succeed in life. They have your best interest at heart. But the course they set out for you is not really you. They might hurt your feelings at the very least and more detrimental, your self-identity. Living some else's life although a great life in certain respects is not the best life and not your life.

Do you really want to be the best feather in the world?

I'm sure you do not because a feather is still a feather whether on purpose or by accident. My friends, life is short, and your viewpoint and subsequent actions will determine if it will be even shorter. Not necessarily in terms of years on this earth but in terms of the quality of time on this earth.

Let me tell you a brief story of two friends. One friend was called "Wherever" and the other the "Greatestever". Both started out as feathers going wherever the wind blew them. These buddies were close. They did everything together. From sunup to sundown, they were inseparable. Weeks turned into months and months into years.

Then one day, Greatestever started to feel differently about himself. As the years went by, he started to watch others enjoy themselves. He saw others being content, flourishing and prospering as opposed to floating with the wind, being slave to a master. Greatestever saw that it was possible to live independently without the wind. Greatestever began sharing his good news with his best friend, Wherever. He talked and talked for days and even weeks to his friend. Hoping to convince his friend that there was a better way for both of them to live. A life of freedom. A rewarding life where they could determine their direction and destination.

Unfortunately, Wherever, never accepted Greatestever's teachings and observations. Then one day Greatestever informed his friend that he was no longer a feather subservient to the wind. Greatestever shared with his friend of his carefully laid out plans to be what he always was but his friend rejected independent thought and wisdom.

Greatestever was sad to see his friend stagnate and stay the same demonstrating no growth and development, although Wherever saw the same things, experienced the same things and felt the same way. The biggest difference between the two friends is one friend acted, and the other did not, deciding to play it safe and stay the same being told what to do, where to go and what to think.

So, do you want to be Greatestever or Wherever?

Now, I referred to family controlling your lives. However, the biggest threat is those that want to control you for selfish and even evil intentions. Remember the movie Thelma and Louise?

Spoiler alert!

At the end of the movie, it did not end well for either of the two primary characters, plunging quite literally to their doom in the Grand Canyon. If you have friends or frenemies, workers, or people that are jealous of you and dislike or even hate you, stay away from them. Realistically, I know this is not always possible. Give them no place in your life. Before, you get engaged, tied up or married, or becoming a business partner let this serve as a beacon of warning to know who you are dealing with before making commitments and promises you shall sooner or later regret.

Watch out for manipulators more accurately coined as controllers. If you don't want to be someone's feather, then don't become one. Do yourself a favor and live your life as the Greatestever!

# 27

# You Know Me

**Dragon of Monophobia (Insecurity)**

In contemplating the title of this chapter about relationships, I thought deeply, more accurately, strangely about the
2000 movie Cast Away Starring Tom Hanks. The film depicts
FedEx employee Chuck Noland (Tom Hanks) stranded on a
remote inhabited island after his plane crashes leaving him
the sole survivor. The only friend Chuck had was Wilson,
no not a living breathing person but just a volleyball. Can
you imagine trapped on a deserted island for four long years
alone with a volleyball as your best friend?

Ouch!

No offense intended to volleyball aficionados.

I am sure you are waiting for the nexus to the topic of
relationships from volleyballs and remote islands.

Okay then, let's get started.

Most if not all human beings long for some type of interaction with others, pets notwithstanding. My argument rest with the need for human interaction. So, for you animal lovers don't take it personal for which I am an animal enthusiast as well.

Back to the movie.

Cast Away wasn't about a herculean superman type conquering the harsh environment he was thrust in but more so how does the typical someone get through days, weeks, months, and years isolated without losing his mind? How does someone cope without a human touch or even a whisper of encouragement? How does he maintain his humanity? How does he have hope let alone faith that everything will be okay? How does he reconcile that his current state of living more than likely will be forever, never to see loved ones and friends ever again? How does he come to terms with the significant negative mental chatter that he's been replaced in the lives of his wife, employer, and others? Chuck was physically and quite literally in a horrible circumstance, fighting regularly for his survival. Being in a Matrix type environment that life is great would be warranted in his case.

You see back home, I'm sure companionship & love, friendship, food, water, clothes, and housing was a given, not on the forefront of his mind as it was expected those things would be there at his disposal. Notice I placed companionship ahead of the typical Maslow's Hierarchy of Needs chart where basic necessities like food, water, clothes are at the essential head of the line.

Personally, if I were abandoned on an island the very first thing, I would think about on day one at the first 30 minutes of being stranded would be I am alone on this XXX island. Moreover, I would self-question, "will I die here alone never to see my wife or family or talk to another human being ever again?" Then and only then would I think of starving to death.

In the absence of the necessities mentioned above, I bet for sure the things for survival earlier taken for granted back home occupied nearly every moment of Chuck's current thoughts, dreams and very existence. But a desire for a relationship was the primary driver. If it were not true that his desire for companionship was one of the most important things in his mind, then please explain Wilson his volleyball buddy?

Despite his predicament he had an emotional, psychological and I believe physiological need to be with someone or he wouldn't have survived. Chuck found those things in Wilson. Apparently, Chuck manufactured in his mind that his volleyball satisfied the parts missing in his life.

In my opinion Wilson was the reason Chuck survived. Let's imagine the setting was different and Chuck was in a civilized society surrounded by thousands of people where there are countless opportunities for relationships of every kind. The dynamics would be centered on normal day living, working, and playing and not hoping to survive one day at a time being besties with a volleyball.

What is my point?

We are Chuck without a doubt. We have the same desire as Chuck did in the film. To simply be wanted and loved at the friendship and/or intimacy level. Although it may be easier to be friends and close with a volleyball not so much with people. Maybe I am cynical, but volleyballs don't involve drama and B.S. As you are aware, people are complicated creatures figuratively and some literally.

Desirable or meaningful personal relationships are difficult to establish and even more challenging to maintain. In my experience and observations over the many years the most important relationships seem to just fall in place organically without little effort. Reflect when you were a child going to school and the recess bell rang.

All the kids seem to come together to play baseball, tag, football, or the game of choice at the time. A few instant friendships were made, true not with everyone as there were and will be cliques. Some friendships had to simmer for a little while before breaking out like a cocoon.

As a child through teenage hood, it seemed we operated under extremes, someone was either your friend or an enemy.

In actuality, and emotion aside, there was a grey area where they were neither because you just didn't cross the same paths or get sufficient opportunity to become friends. Yet, life as a kid was much easier than life as an adult. Of course, bad things happened as a child or teenager. Everything was not perfect or at times even okay.

Now forwarding to adulthood, life gets more complicated in terms of everything including relationships. Unfortunately, we carry that childhood baggage into adulthood. I think we focused more on the negative versus the teachings we learned that could be applied as an adult saving us countless hours on connecting with people, rather the wrong people to be most accurate.

A one size doesn't fit all when it comes to a discussion on this topic. Nevertheless, there is commonalities that we can draw upon. Let's start with basic friendships. In short, we want a friend that has a similar viewpoint. Someone that see's the world as we see it. Of course, they don't have to be hundred percent in agreement, just enough to get along with each other and enjoy the time. We want a friend to talk about our problems, our victories, and our struggles. A supportive friend that will cheerlead us on and be there when things get tough and celebrate when things are great. A friend that won't be like a vampire and suck the positive energy draining us of life, time, and money.

What about more than friends?

Intimacy is the hope and desire many people wish or pray for in this life. Companies like Eharmony, Match.com and Bumble's business is to help find you that perfect someone. These companies make millions to billions of dollars hoping to get it right. Of course, there are the other places that in my opinion people bottom fish like night clubs, bars, and other venues. Whatever the source the intention is to discover companionship, love or just physical encounters which disguise themselves as real love or basic friendship.

When looking for love, most people want the same things written above regarding friendships. Someone that is supportive and has many things in common with you. Again, it's okay to have some differences they just cannot be the big things, i.e., money, behavioral, major dislikes etc.

Just like friendships you cannot force love on anyone. It either organically happens or you force it. If it's forced and you're hoping and praying but it's not there, I wish you well. Walking in a minefield blindfolded is what it appears to be. Don't dismiss the red flags and rely on pure emotion. Self-deception is unbelievably bad. Before you know it you just wasted five, ten and even twenty years of precious life on the wrong person.

Unfortunately, I can write from experience. We only had a couple of things truly in common. It was convenient and pleasant at first. Then true colors came out over a period of time. A very selfish and self-centered person. I now am with my best friend that truly has our best interest at heart. Noticed I said our as we are true partners in every way.

Final point about relationships, people may be in your life for only a season or certain period of time. Relationships may refer to intimate relationships or friendships. Just think back on friends you had while in school or work friends that vanished after you left the job. What about hobby friends. You know like bowling or poker friends. They are there while you engage in whatever activity.

In terms of finding real love, take your time don't force it and don't engage in certain behavior too soon before you are ready. Things may seem great now, but haste makes waste. All of us was young and stupid once or twice don't make it thrice. Love is like a slow brewing coffee, it takes time, so give it time.

# 28

# The Faucet

**Dragon of Anthropophobia**
**(Fear of People)**

The faucet is a remarkable thing. I can't imagine my life without it. Much like magic, you move a lever then miraculously water flows from it. Can you even contemplate what the repercussions would be if the faucet suddenly vanished from every home in the United States and every modernized home in the world?

Anarchy! Civil War! The sky is falling! The end is near. May be dramatic but I'm just saying.

Homestratosphere.com reported interesting facts. The faucet has been around since 1000 B.C. The Ancient Romans used silver faucets. However, if you are talking about the modern faucet then a gentleman with the name of Alfred Moen invented a single-handed faucet that blended cold and hot water in 1937. His invention was subsequently improved upon by others as time went on. Twenty-two years later from its invention, Alfred Moen's single-handed faucets were in almost every home.

Prior to its invention, the retrieval of water was rather challenging. Although, we must give credit to the plumbing that goes along with it as well. Anyhow, they had to use buckets or barrels to transport water to its destination which mostly was for Domestic reasons. Wells were a main source way back when but still around today all over the world.

Think about the time it saves you as the water comes to you. We bathe, clean our dirty dishes, wash our clothes, clean our vehicles, water the trees, lawn, flowers and plants and drink from it. Of course, there are many more uses for the faucet, but you get the idea. Okay, thank you for indulging with me on my fascination with this simple yet remarkable invention.

Although the faucet is great, and is a much-needed tool, better yet is what it represents and symbolizes. It serves as analogy or is symbolic for each of us to be the encouraging and uplifting water pouring out of our faucet to fill someone else's bucket. Not to give away my age, I have lived long enough to witness and experience the good in people and the worst in them.

If everyone would take an internal pledge of simply being humane and just be nice to others much of the conflict we see would go away. We don't have to like each other just respect each other for being a human being that is born into rights we seem to have to fight for on a daily basis. Encouraging and building up one another is most productive and positively life altering. Building up versus tearing down is my anthem.

Although, I can take this discussion to a stratospheric level I want to bring it down to earth. The fact is there are many people around us going through challenges that impact their ability to cope with their circumstances or just life in general. Many people suffer from depression, some more severe than others. Depression can steal the enjoyments of life and even a life itself.

What is depression?

According to the Mao Clinic: "Depression is a mood disorder that causes a persistent feeling of sadness and loss of interest. Also called major depressive disorder or clinical depression, it affects how you feel, think, and behave and can lead to a variety of emotional and physical problems. You may have trouble doing normal day-to-day activities, and sometimes you may feel as if life isn't worth living."

The number of people that suffer from depression is huge. According to the World Healthcare Organization (WHO) estimates that more than **300 million** people worldwide suffer from depression. Moreover, the WHO also states it is the world's leading cause of disability. That said, besides families and friends, employers and many businesses are recipients of the magnitude depression has on employees resulting in an impact felt on a societal level.

We don't know what people are going through that we work with, go to school, shop at the store, and perhaps live with as family members or otherwise. What I'm saying is the people I am speaking about can be strangers or equally as common as a child, spouse, siblings, or other personal ties.

Life is tough as it is without pointing a single finger of blame to a root cause. My point is we should not add to or create unnecessary strife or negativity to others. However, if we were to point a laser beam focused finger that finger would point to abusers, either physical or emotional. An example is all to unfortunately familiar- bullying. Bullies are people being at their worst either in the playground at school or the playground at the job. What compounds this serious issue is the people and organizations that witness it and do not nothing or too little to stop it or prevent it. We have racist bullies, domestic bullies, school bullies, job bullies, religious bullies, political bullies and so forth.

This chapter was not intended to be a full dissertation on the negative effect of depression as it relates to the evils of bullying, just exposing it in my way for the benefit of those going through depression and/or bullying or those helping others get through their challenges.

Unfortunately, I have experienced bullies involving three of the above but like many others as well. Bullying is linked in many ways to the depression of its victims. In many instances this is on top of possible underlying issues prior to the bullying even taking place. It could be the root cause or exacerbated because of bullying.

Yes, there are other causes or contributors of depression. Depression may be caused by a life changing event such as a death in the family, addiction or loss of a job. These can be emotionally draining and also financially detrimental which can cause someone to spiral out of control. You don't have to have a propensity for it because of genetic factors or prone to experiencing depression. All it takes is one small incident to ignite it. To clarify, one small incident in reality but not small perceptively to the victim of depression.

Symptoms

"Although depression may occur only once during your life, people typically have multiple episodes. During these episodes, symptoms occur most of the day, nearly every day and may include:

- Feelings of sadness, tearfulness, emptiness, or hopelessness
- Angry outbursts, irritability or frustration, even over small matters

- Loss of interest or pleasure in most or all normal activities, such as sex, hobbies or sports
- Sleep disturbances, including insomnia or sleeping too much
- Tiredness and lack of energy, so even small tasks take extra effort
- Reduced appetite and weight loss or increased cravings for food and weight gain
- Anxiety, agitation or restlessness
- Slowed thinking, speaking or body movements
- Feelings of worthlessness or guilt, fixating on past failures or self-blame
- Trouble thinking, concentrating, making decisions and remembering things
- Frequent or recurrent thoughts of death, suicidal thoughts, suicide attempts or suicide
- Unexplained physical problems, such as back pain or headaches"

Depression and symptom information source: Mayo Clinic.

If you believe you have depression and/or experience suicidal thoughts call the suicide hotline number: **Call 911 if immediate emergency. National Suicide Prevention Lifeline** at 1-800-273-TALK (1-800-273-8255). If you are veteran or the family/friend of a veteran, use that same number and press "1" to reach the Veterans Crisis Line. If you don't mind this advice, please contact a friend or a trusted family member or mentor at your religious or nonreligious affiliation if you have challenges coping with whatever is on your mind.

I am a survivor and so are you if this pertains to you. May peace and a long fruitful life be with you.

**P.S.** don't stand idly by as someone is being bullied report it and do the right thing. Please visit **Stopbullying.gov or call (800) 273-8255 or 911 if immediate emergency.**

## 29

# Planting Your Seed

**Dragon of Botanophobia (Fear of Plants)**

Your top priority is to invest in yourself. We are much like plants requiring food and water to flourish, grow and quite literally to survive. Investing in one's self is not meant to splurge on frivolity but to consider yourself important for yourself, your family, friends and to the world. For many people it is very hard to focus attention on ourselves.

We think of everyone else but fail to include ourselves. We sacrifice for our children, our partners and even complete strangers but omit one vital person. What I am saying is not revolutionary or selfish at all. My late mother was the most generous giving soul that ever existed, helping numerous people and institutions that were in the business of helping others.

Sad to say, on many occasions, she left her self out of the equation, never splurging adequately for herself and on her self as much as she deserved. You see we were meant to enjoy this thing called life as well; not just living our lives through the lens of others all the time. Spend some time living for yourself. I'm not inferring to be narcissistic and to not help others but sufficiently participate in our own lives. Redirect some resources back to you. Again, don't be neglectful to your family and others who we should morally help. You don't have to be rich today in order to plant the seedlings that will bring you overwhelming prosperity tomorrow. Like the mighty oak it all starts with a small seed.

Planting your seed also refers to protecting your health. This is a high priority because if your health is not good then all the material things this life has to offer will not mean anything. Your education or income will be in jeopardy. Therefore, eating well, exercise and staying emotionally fit should be of top focus.

In terms of relationships, connecting with someone that will be your true partner working with you every step of the way on your level will propel you faster and on a larger scale. This isn't an absolute necessity for success as single people will be just fine all alone. Being alone does not equate to being lonely. The point is if you were to be in a relationship with a significant other, be with someone that is in your best interest. Otherwise, you will be dragged down by an anchor so heavy you will prolong your achievements and the success you deserve longer than necessary.

In terms of relationships, you should have common

interests, desires, beliefs, and motivations. They say opposites attract. Only to a small degree of being opposite. It usually does not turn out well where there is large Grand Canyon like crater differences. You will have wasted time which you can never get back, wasted energy like being sucked by a vampire or vacuum cleaner and wasted money and resources traveling down a path not meant to be traveled. Horrible idea but do what you must. Re-read my chapter on "How'd That Work out for You".

That seed for you to plant could take the form of education, either academic or vocational. Your source of income akin to revenue for a business. The other manifestations of planting your seed won't materialize if you don't have a reliable income. And to establish that income require some degree of learning and sacrifice. The more you know and can apply the greater the possibility of earning a higher income to support yourself and your own family.

As your income grows planting your seed in investments such as stocks, index funds, exchange traded funds, real estate and business will take you to even greater financial heights. The key here is to start early and consistent. Your money grows by compounding, appreciating, and generating dividends. I encourage you to read books on this matter and visit various YouTube channels that provide excellent educational material. I highly encourage you to subscribe to our podcast and channels, RaisingTheKane , go to RaisingTheKane.com.

Many wealthy people became wealthy from starting a

business. If you have an idea or passion that you believe has merit and that may sustain you then do your research on the Internet, asks a lot of questions from experts, coaches, and mentors, and go for it if that is in your spirit to do. I am more than ready, willing and able to coach you so that you may determine what is right for you.

In closing, I wish you well in your pursuits. Don't live a life of regret wishing you would have tried something but didn't. Jump in with both eyes open and watch those scammers, 'trust but verify", a quote from President Reagan. That quote has served me well. Well, keep your mind open to the possibilities. And finally, live your own life but sensibly planned of course not relying on others. There is a time to adventure conquering the unknown country so to speak. I hope I was able to impart useful information to you. I also hope I was able to plant a seed in your life.

# 30

## Bonus Chapter

**Your Emotional Intelligence Journey**

I received part of my inspiration for this chapter from Gill Hasson author of Emotional Intelligence (E.I.) and John Campbell an American mythologist, writer, and lecturer.

The emotional intelligence journey is not an easy one. It's full of twists, curves, dips, and climbs. It can be elusive for sure if you are not aware of managing it.

What is Emotional Intelligence?

According to Wikipedia, "Emotional intelligence (EI) is most often defined as the ability to perceive, use, understand, manage, and handle emotions. People with high emotional intelligence can recognize their own emotions and those of others, use emotional information to guide thinking and behavior, discern between different feelings and label them appropriately, and adjust emotions to adapt to environments. Although the term first appeared in 1964, it gained popularity in the 1995 best-selling book Emotional Intelligence, written by science journalist Daniel Goleman. Goleman defined EI as the array of skills and characteristics that drive leadership performance."

Emotions are made up of actions, physical feelings, and thoughts. Notice I did not say control emotions or be controlling or manipulative. The point of E.I.in your personal life or in the workplace is to make a positive impact on your employees, supervisors and on you and your career and also your life in general.

Whether we're at the job or the store, wherever we go, we are likely interacting with other people. These interactions are usually either positive or negative. In fact, our lives are a series of presentations, albeit, mostly informal. We are either attempting to share information or requesting something from someone or providing something to someone free of charge or a cost associated with the interaction.

That cost maybe monetary in nature or an investment or cost of your time. E.I. can benefit anyone desirous of career advancement and/or improving their working relationships with peers and others. If you are retired or non-working this is great for you as well. Learning how to navigate the world of people. If your only ambition is making friends and influencing people that's okay to. E.I. will help bring peace and contentment to your life if nothing else.

Since many if not most of us spend the majority of our time at work, I will focus the E.I. conversation in the context of our working lives. Although, this discussion is applicable anywhere you are interacting with people. Additionally, the term leader is interchangeable with employee as I view all employees as leaders, with little "l" or big "L", essentially one and the same.

The E.I. journey in this case is not necessarily literal like the one we're on traveling on vacation or to work. See definitions below. So figuratively your spirit, your thoughts, your whole mindset and resulting behavior and actions must take a journey from "Who you are today", i.e., the neophyte leader, the sort of growing leader, the insecure leader, the lukewarm leader, the cookie cutter leader meaning the status Quo leader (not changing staying the same do what everyone does). So, coming from the old land to the new land, the promise land i.e., the effective leader, the inspirational leader, the visionary leader you want to become.

Journey defined:

1. Traveling from one place to another
2. A voyage
3. Drive
4. Excursion
5. Expedition

6. Mindset

So, to develop as a leader consistently and purposefully you must pack your bags and pay the price for the expedition, the journey. Attending workshops, classes and attending seminars and reading books, volunteering to take on greater responsibilities and perhaps promotional opportunities etc. In the end the journey I am speaking about is first in your "head- most accurately in your mind".

Emotional Intelligence Definition: the ability to understand and manage your emotions and others.

| Limbic System | Neo-Cortex |
|---|---|
| Emotional Responses | Conscious Thought |
| Simple and Basic | Complex Mental activities |
| Intuition | Rational Thinking |
| React | Reasoning |
| Respond Quickly | Responder Slower |

Refer to chart above:

Definition. **Limbic System** – you're walking in the crosswalk and a car is speeding at you, not stopping. You jump out of the way. Or, a snake pops out of nowhere as you hike on a trail. You exhibit fear and run. Was that an emotional response or (neo-cortex) did you wait for a moment to think about it or spend minutes rationalizing your potential reactions?

Intuition – The process that gives you the ability to know something directly without thinking. inner voice telling you something. It's being aware of 5 senses, i.e., taste, hear, see, smell and touch. Something doesn't feel right (unusual or out of place). Be open to all messages your intuition is communicating.

Five Elements of emotional intelligence:

1. Self-awareness
2. Self-regulation
3. Motivation
4. Empathy
5. Social Skills

**Self-awareness** – acknowledge and recognize to yourself your behaviors that you are exhibiting. Know how you're feeling. Know your strengths and weaknesses. Evaluate your thought patterns in situations especially those challenging, i.e., performance discussions, potential disciplinary actions. Measure your reactions when engaging with others.

**Self-Regulation** – Staying in control, know your values, code of ethics, be calm.

**Motivation** – More important than trying to motivate someone else, is self-motivation which lasts the other does not. You have a stake in the game when you tell yourself I want to do my best and be my best. The result is high standards, your quality goes up and your productivity. Your professional relationships get better. And you are optimistic – a bright and shiny outlook on life and your future.

**Empathy** – Compassion for others is what makes us human. I have met some people over many years such as rank & file staff and high-level managers in important leadership roles that demonstrated none unfortunately, but thankfully most people have it. You should be open or flexible to under-standing others' plight. Wearing another person's shoes so to speak. The point is to work with others as you navigate the world of work and begin or continue your leadership journey.

**Social skills** – As a leader, how we communicate with others reflect how they perceive us. Praise others. Acknowl-edge others. It's not always about you. Resolving conflicts in a way where there's a win-win as opposed to a win-I can't wait to destroy you. Let others as well as yourself keep your dignity. I highly recommend a good book – "How to Win Friends and influence people" Dale Carnegie.

Six Basic Emotions

- Fear
- Anger = Contempt = rage/Loathing
- Disgust

- Surprise
- Sadness
- Joy

Basic emotions can join or blend into each other to form complex emotions. For example, the emotions anger and disgust blended together breed "contempt". To make things more explosive left uncontrolled the next level after anger is rage and loathing from disgust. Thus, it is important to manager your emotions to not allow things to get worse. If things can get worse, they will if you remain passive.

Taking Responsibility for your emotions:

1. She made me angry
2. He embarrassed me
3. If you …… I wouldn't have ……

"She made me angry". "He embarrassed me". Own your emotions. You create the emotions you are experiencing. You possess the power. Unmet needs become emotional triggers. When negative emotions are involved be slow to speak, write or act. Quote – "Emotions say hurry. Wisdom says wait."

Emotional triggers:

- Disobedient child
- Failed to accomplish goals
- Criticism from spouse or partner

- Missing an important event
- Your team didn't win
- Date night: forgot wallet after eating dinner

**What about positive triggers?**

Example, your birthday. Wedding day. Honeymoon time … hmmm. Received pay raise. Got that big promotion.
Increasing your E.I.

- Assertive
- Active listening
- Reframing
- Think before you talk
- Self-Talk
- Empathy
- Assertive – demonstrating courage, be heard, be understood.
- Active listening - listen to understand not to respond.
- Reframing- changing the way you think.
- Think- gather thoughts, use reason.
- Self-talk- eliminate the glass is always empty thinking. See the positive. Understanding their plight, what they are experiencing.
- Empathy – managing other disappointments.

# Appendix I

**Diary of Freedom**

# Appendix II

**Phobias**

Acarophobia- Fear of itching or of the insects that cause itching.

Acerophobia- Fear of sourness.

Achluophobia- Fear of darkness.

Acousticophobia- Fear of noise.

Acrophobia- Fear of heights.

Aerophobia- Fear of swallowing,

Androphobia – Fear of men.

Barophobia- Fear of gravity.

Basophobia- Inability to stand. Fear of walking or falling.

Bathmophobia- Fear of stairs or steep slopes.

Bathophobia- Fear of depth.

Batophobia- Fear of heights or being close to high buildings.

Batrachophobia- Fear of amphibians, such as frogs, newts, salamanders, etc.

Belonephobia- Fear of pins and needles. (Aichmophobia)

Bibliophobia- Fear of books.

Blennophobia- Fear of slime.

Bogyphobia- Fear of bogeys or the bogeyman.

Botanophobia- Fear of plants.


Cacophobia- Fear of ugliness.


Cainophobia- Fear of newness, novelty.

Cancerophobia or Carcinophobia- Fear of cancer.

Cardiophobia- Fear of the heart.


Carnophobia- Fear of meat.

Catagelophobia- Fear of being ridiculed.

Catapedaphobia- Fear of jumping from high and low places.

Cathisophobia- Fear of sitting.

Catoptrophobia- Fear of mirrors.


Decidophobia- Fear of making decisions.


Demonophobia or Daemonophobia- Fear of demons.

Demophobia- Fear of crowds. (Agoraphobia)

Dendrophobia- Fear of trees.

Dentophobia- Fear of dentists.

Dermatophobia- Fear of skin lesions.

Dermatosiophobia- Fear of skin disease.

Dextrophobia- Fear of objects at the right side of the body.

Diabetophobia- Fear of diabetes.

Didaskaleinophobia- Fear of going to school.


Dikephobia – Fear of justice.


Epistemophobia – Fear of knowledge.

Gallophobia - Fear France or French culture. (Franco-phobia).

Gamophobia- Fear of marriage.

Geliophobia- Fear of laughter.

Geniophobia- Fear of chins.

Hagiophobia- Fear of saints or holy things.

Hamartophobia- Fear of sinning.

Haphephobia - Fear of being touched.

Harpaxophobia- Fear of being robbed.

Heliophobia- Fear of the sun.

Hellenologophobia- Fear of Greek terms or complex scientific terminology.

Helminthophobia- Fear of being infested with worms.

Hemophobia - Fear of blood.

Herpetophobia- Fear of reptiles or creepy, crawly things.

Heterophobia- Fear of the opposite sex. (Sexophobia)

Hexakosioihexekontahexaphobia- Fear of the number 666.

Hierophobia- Fear of priests or sacred things.

Hippophobia- Fear of horses.

Hippopotomonstrosesquipedaliophobia- Fear of long words.

Hobophobia- Fear of bums or beggars.

Hodophobia- Fear of road travel.

Hormephobia- Fear of shock.

Homichlophobia- Fear of fog.

Homilophobia- Fear of sermons.

Hominophobia- Fear of men.

Homophobia- Fear of sameness, monotony or of.

Hoplophobia- Fear of firearms.

Hydrargyophobia- Fear of mercurial medicines.

Hydrophobia- Fear of water or of rabies.

Hydrophobophobia- Fear of rabies.

Hyelophobia - Fear of glass.

Hygrophobia- Fear of liquids, dampness, or moisture.

Hylephobia- Fear of materialism or the fear of epilepsy.

Hylophobia- Fear of forests.

Hypengyophobia - Fear of responsibility.

Hypnophobia- Fear of sleep or of being hypnotized.

Hypsiphobia- Fear of height.


Lachanophobia – Fear of vegetables.


Ichthyophobia- Fear of fish.

Ideophobia- Fear of ideas.

Illyngophobia- Fear of feeling dizzy when looking down.

Iophobia- Fear of poison.

Insectophobia - Fear of insects.

Isolophobia- Fear of being alone.

Isopterophobia- Fear of termites, insects that eat wood.


jcatapedaphobia – Fear of jumping.


Maniaphobia – Fear of madness.

Mechanophobia – Fear of machinery.

Mnemophobia – Fear of memories


Nebulaphobia- Fear of fog.

Necrophobia- Fear of death or dead things.

Nelophobia- Fear of glass.

Neopharmaphobia- Fear of new drugs.

Neophobia- Fear of anything new.
Nephophobia- Fear of clouds.Oenophobia - Fear of wine.


Omphalophobia- Fear of belly buttons.
Oneirophobia- Fear of dreams.

Pharmacophobia – Fear of medicine.
Peccatiphobia – Fear of wrongdoing.
Philemaphobia – Fear of kissing.
Plutophobia – Fear of wealth.
Primeisodophobia – Fear of losing one's virginity.

Radiophobia- Fear of radiation, x-rays.
Ranidaphobia- Fear of frogs.
Rhabdophobia – Fear of magic.
Rhytiphobia – Fear of getting wrinkles.

Scoleciphobia – Fear of worms.
Scriptophobia – Fear of writing in public.
Spheksophobia-Fear of wasps.

Tabophobia – Fear of wasting sickness.

Vaccinophobia – Fear of vaccination.

Xenoglossophobia- Fear of foreign languages.

Xenophobia- Fear of strangers or foreigners.

Xerophobia- Fear of dryness.

Zelophobia – Fear of jealousy.

Zemmiphobia- Fear of the great mole rat.

**Http://phobialist.com / Dictionary.com/ Fearof.net**

# Appendix III

## Positive Cookies

1. You will dream of success when you do aim high.
2. There are two mirrors of your life, one in front of you the other behind you, learn from the rear mirror but be led, by the mirror in front of you.
3. Choose your friends carefully, measure their intentions wisely and believe their actions truthfully.
4. Stay on the path that you set for yourself, so prosperity may find you sooner versus later.
5. Your spouse or significant other will either bless you or betray you if you choose someone not aligned to your purpose.
6. Even animals understand their role, learn from them, and move toward your goals.
7. Learn, observe, and act and you will be what you desire.
8. Earn, save, invest, and spend wisely and money will never be an issue.
9. Peace is around the corner when you accept things as they are but push forward embracing what could be.

10. The warrior in you is waiting to get out to conquer the world but first you must conquer your heart.

11. Time is the most precious commodity. It cannot be planted, grown or harvested but can be treasured.

12. Vision is about seeing things clearly. Like a car with foggy windows, you will after you turn the wiper blades on in your mind, wiping away the confusion.

13. Life is finite, so live every day as your birthday, enjoy and celebrate and focus on the have's not the have nots.

14. Be the author of your own story don't be a feather being controlled by the ever- changing wind of others.

15. Rise up to the challenges of life, you're as talented, as smart and courageous as the next person.

16. Put your team to work, your spirit, your mind, and your body. They will guide you according to your wishes and goals.

17. Plant seeds in others so they may benefit from your experience and wisdom and grow like a forest that started with only one tree.

18. Health matters, without it nothing else will matter.

19. When things get tough, and they will, don't quit believing in yourself, demonstrate who you are meant to be, prove them wrong.

20. You are powerful. You are strong. You are successful.

# Appendix IV

**Positive Mind Chatter**

You will dream of success when you do aim high.

There are two mirrors of your life, one in front of you the other behind you, learn from the rear mirror but be led, by the mirror in front of you.

Choose your friends carefully, measure their intentions wisely and believe their actions truthfully.

Stay on the path that you set for yourself, so prosperity may find you sooner versus later.

Your spouse or significant other will either bless you or betray you if you choose someone not aligned to your purpose.

Even animals understand their role, learn from them and move toward your goals.

Learn, observe, and act and you will be what you desire.

Earn, save, invest, and spend wisely and money will never be an issue.

Peace is around the corner when you accept things as they are but push forward embracing what could be.

The warrior in you is waiting to get out to conquer the world but first you must conquer your heart.

Time is the most precious commodity. It cannot be planted, grown or harvested but can be treasured.

Vision is about seeing things clearly. Like a car with foggy windows, you will see clearly after you turn the wiper blades on in your mind, wiping away the confusion.

Life is finite, so live every day as your birthday, enjoy and celebrate and focus on the have's not the have nots.

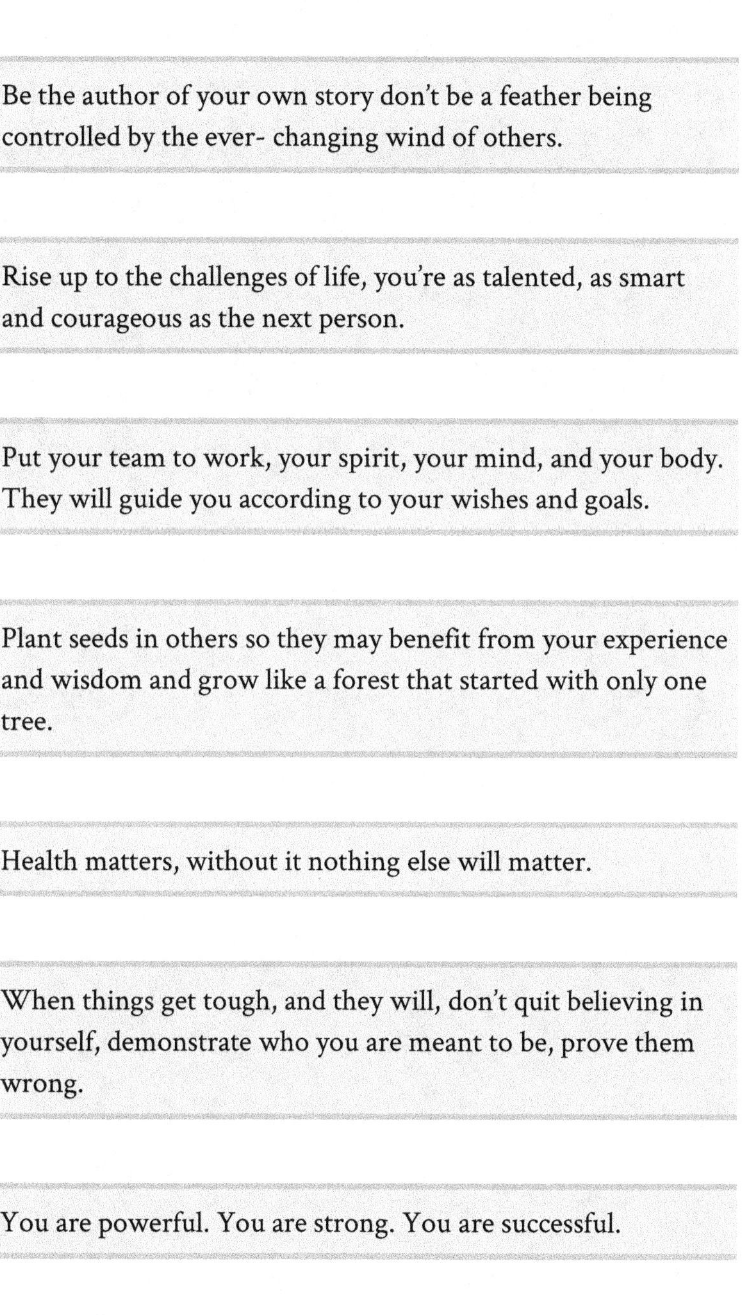

Be the author of your own story don't be a feather being controlled by the ever- changing wind of others.

Rise up to the challenges of life, you're as talented, as smart and courageous as the next person.

Put your team to work, your spirit, your mind, and your body. They will guide you according to your wishes and goals.

Plant seeds in others so they may benefit from your experience and wisdom and grow like a forest that started with only one tree.

Health matters, without it nothing else will matter.

When things get tough, and they will, don't quit believing in yourself, demonstrate who you are meant to be, prove them wrong.

You are powerful. You are strong. You are successful.

# A Coaching Moment

**The self-assessment is meant for you to learn more about yourself. The goal is for you to be proactive in your quest to get out of life those things you only dream about and not realized yet.**

### Self-Awareness Assessment

1. If you could recreate the earth, what would it look like?
2. If you could live another 100 years or more, would you?
3. I do my best in every activity or job.
4. I have confidence in myself no matter the situation.
5. I am open to seeking advice from others.
6. I set high standards for myself.
7. I allow fear to control my thoughts or actions.
8. Fear has prevented me from living the life I always wanted.
9. I will never realize my goals.
10. I am optimistic about tomorrow.
11. Motivation comes naturally to me.

12. Procrastination stops me from achieving my dreams.
13. I get dissatisfied quite easily.
14. I maintain a healthy lifestyle.
15. I need to make changes to my eating habits.
16. I exercise regularly.
17. I save sufficient money for any emergencies.
18. I save a portion of my paycheck to purchase items in cash for the future.
19. I earn enough money to maintain a comfortable lifestyle.
20. I am an initiator.
21. I passively follow.
22. I am undecisive.
23. I give myself gifts or special treats.
24. I cannot stop mulling over regrets from poor decisions.
25. I don't see a bright future for myself.
26. I feel lonely most of the time.
27. I wish I could push a reset button on my life and start over.
28. I have family or friends to confide my woes.
29. I wish I had a coach or mentor to guide me.
30. I am on the right path with my life.
31. I need to start making changes quickly.
32. I help others in some manner or form.
33. Time management is not my issue.
34. I wish I had a magic wand.
35. Negative chatter takes over my mind.
36. I am open to learning new things,
37. I want to improve my life.
38. I have a definite plan for retirement.
39. I spend my time with hobbies.
40. I have close friends.

41. I know what I want in life.
42. I believe luck is the only way to achieve my goals.
43. If you could speak to someone that passed on who would that be?
44. I have all the courage I need to be successful.
45. I like to win at everything.
46. I resent others.
47. I am angry about a situation or someone.
48. I feel betrayed.
49. If I only had ______, I would do ______
50. I am honest with myself.

# Special Offers

Do Something About It!

- Do you want to get ahead but find yourself on that hamster wheel going nowhere?
- Ending where you started?
- Are you tired of being tired?
- Peace of mind, good health and prosperity eluding you?

Then, we may have what you need.
We offer the following services:

- Coaching
- Retreats
- Hypnotherapy

Buying this book will entitle you to discounts!!!
Please visit www.livingyoursuccess.com

# Say ...

**Say Goodbye**

"Say Goodbye to the Destroyer of Goals and Dreams"


**Say Hello**

"Say hello to the Builder of Success and Achievement"

# The Author

Michael Kane is a transformation coach helping clients define and achieve their personal, professional, and business goals. He is the author of "Slaying Your Dragons, Living the Life you Always Wanted." He is a motivational speaker, entrepreneur and host and cohost of two podcasts, Living Your Success and  RaisingTheKane that can be heard on Apple, iHeart, Spotify, Amazon Music and many more networks and channels.